SCOTTISH

Myths and Legends

SCOTTISH

Myths and Legends

JUDY HAMILTON

WAVERLEY BOOKS

Published 2009 by Waverley Books,
David Dale House,
New Lanark, ML11 9DJ, Scotland

© 2009 Waverley Books

ISBN 978 1 902407 84 5

Printed and bound in the UK

contents

introduction 7
tales of the sea 10
 assispattle and the stoorworm 12
 the crofter and the seal-woman 26
 the seal hunter's lesson 30
 the seal of sule skerry 34
 the mermaid's revenge 36
 two tales of the blue men 39
Legendary places 44
 the gold of Largo Law 44
 the chatter of the birds: how eilean donan was
  built 46
 the Legend of corryvreckan 50
 smoo cave 52
 the swans of Loch sunart 54
 the saving of the forest 56
monsters on Land and in water 60
 the Loch ness monster 60
 morag of Loch morar 64
 the Linton worm 67
 michael scott and the serpent 70
 the big grey man of ben macdhui 76
visitors to the fairy realm 82
 thomas the rhymer 83
 what happened to the reverend robert kirk? 87
 the fiddlers of tomnahurich 89
Legendary figures 92
 rob roy macgregor and macalpine of clan grant 92
 bruce and the spider 95
 claverhouse warned 97
 the brahan seer 99

celtic myths of heroes and fair maids   104
    deidre of the sorrows   104
    diarmid and grainne   110
    finn saves the children of the big young hero
      and finds bran   115
giant lore   120
    the morvern giant   121
    the tormented gantess   124
    finlay and the giants   127
deadly disturbances   135
    the minister's wife   136
    the living dead   139
witches   143
    the witch of laggan   144
    the fisherman and the witches   150
    the hunter and the hare   153
murder most foul   155
    the legend of sawney bean   155
    the murder hole   159
tales of the clans   167
    the loch of the sword   167
    the faerie flag of the clan macleod   169
    the war of the one-eyed woman   174
holy men of scotland   176
    saint fillan of glen dochart   176
    saint mungo   178
    saint andrew   180
the glaistig and the kelpie   182
    the glaistig of ardnadrochit   184
    the glaistig's curse   184
    the kelpie of loch garve   187
    the killing of the kelpie of raasay   188

introduction

Scotland is a nation made from many peoples and cultures. Through gradual small-scale migration and conquest over many centuries, this country became home to a multi-ethnic population, which was not united until the ninth century AD when Kenneth MacAlpin became the first king of Scots. From prehistoric times, Scotland absorbed elements of culture and language from diverse peoples who came from France, Spain, Central Europe and Scandinavia. The Romans, who first crossed into Scotland in 80AD, abandoned hope of conquering Scotland after more than two hundred years of trying, but their presence left its mark on the inhabitants. The spread of Christianity from the fourth century onwards, the colonisation of Argyll by the Scots from Ireland in the fifth century, the Norse invasions of the ninth century, and the shifting ownership of the territories to the south, all added ingredients to the melting pot of Scotland's culture.

This diversity of cultural influence is reflected in Scotland's vast store of myths and legends. The tales of the Fians, a mythical race of Irish heroes, have crossed the Irish Sea and found a second home in Scotland. Fabulous creatures such as the mermaid and the selkie are shared between Scotland, Ireland and Scandinavia, and have provided material for some of Scotland's favourite ballads and stories. The kelpie is only one of a number of supernatural beings who animate the folklore of both Ireland and Scotland. There are elements in a great number of Scots legends that feature in the story-telling traditions of many countries – man-eating monsters, heroic princes, magic and miraculous feats.

Scotland's turbulent history has also contributed to the richness and variety of its stock of legends. Historical events and the lives of prominent people have been kept alive in the minds of generations of Scots thanks to the skills of the sennachie, or story-teller, and the stories that have been told have added another dimension to these events and people. Few of these stories were ever written down until many generations after their first telling. Scotland's story-telling tradition was primarily an oral one, and story-telling as a form of entertainment at social gatherings retained its popularity, particularly in the Highlands and Islands, until relatively recent times. Stories were passed on from one generation to the next by word of mouth, and their telling was a particular skill. In the case of stories that have been built around people and events of the past, the need for historical accuracy has, more often than not, been considered less important than the need to tell a good story well. Fact and fiction have often become blurred, and sometimes, fact has been obscured. The value of the story is not to be found in the facts.

This book contains a very small selection from Scotland's vast stock of myths and legends. The origins of some of them are obscure, whilst others are based (however loosely) on historical fact. Some tales are very old indeed, whilst others date from later times. Some of the legends – notably that of the Loch Ness Monster – are still evolving. Some tales are very well known, others less so, and readers may find that they have heard versions of some of the stories that are similar in some respects but different in others. There are tales from the Highlands and Lowlands, north, south, east and west. It is not the purpose of this book to attempt any serious analysis of the ages, origins or sources of these stories. This book is intended to provide entertainment for its readers, giving them a small taste of the feast of stories that our country has to offer and tempting them to go in search of more.

tales of the sea

Throughout history, many of the people of Scotland have made their living from the sea. The waters around the coast of Scotland can be treacherous and the weather harsh and unpredictable, and none are more aware of the dangers that they face than those who sail these waters. Given the many hazards of their occupation, it is not surprising that Scottish fisherfolk and sailors have always been superstitious. It is a trait that they share with seafaring people all over the world. The legends about the mysteries that lie beneath the seas around the globe have many features in common, and it is not only in Scotland that tales of man's encounters with creatures of the deep are told. There are two broad categories of creature that feature in these stories. The first category includes a variety of harmful creatures, some monstrous, that put the lives of seafarers in peril by causing storms, sinking ships, blowing vessels off course, and so on. The second category, to which mermaids and seal people belong, are creatures which have been said not only to interact with human beings, but from time to time, to have interbred with them.

Sea monsters feature in legends the world over. They are blamed for missing ships, unexpected storms and mysterious drownings. Some can emerge from their watery lair and cause devastation on land. The Orcadian story of Assispattle and the Stoorworm tells of an epic struggle against a monster of hideously gigantic proportions. Dragons and serpents feature in numerous Scottish folk tales. Many of these creatures are said to live on land,

and when they are slain, they leave their mark on the countryside, in volcanoes, the contours of hillsides, etc. But the Stoorworm is a sea-dwelling serpent, and so great a monster that its death changes the geography of several countries and the waters that surround them. Assispattle's exploits are related in a number of Ordcadian legends. This tale contains many elements common to myths, folktales and fairy tales from various parts of the world. The Stoorworm, like the Minotaur slain by Theseus, is fed with the flesh of the nation's youth. The young hero Assispattle has much in common with Cinderella. Dirty and unkempt, he lives a life of drudgery, sorely mistreated by his family. In slaying the Stoorworm, he is transformed from hapless wretch to noble hero, saviour of a princess and a kingdom. The tale ends, predictably, with the hero marrying the fair princess.

Many people will think of the mermaid as a fabulous creature formed by the imagination of Hans Anderson, whose story of the Little Mermaid is widely known. But in times gone by, mermaids were believed to be real. With a human head and torso and a fish tail, mer-people, and in particular mermaids, were allegedly sighted at various coastal sites around Scotland on numerous occasions over many years. In Scandinavia, belief in mermaids took hold a very long time ago, and in Scotland too, stories of the mer-folk date back over centuries. Many a fisherman has allegedly fallen for the charms of one of these fabulous creatures and few of their stories have happy endings.

The seal-folk, silkies or selkies as they are known in Scotland, resemble ordinary seals while in the water and change into human form when they come ashore and shed their skins. It was widely believed, not only in Scotland but also in Ireland and Scandinavia that seals were in fact humans, who had been put under a spell. Most of the time, it was said, these people were condemned to live as seals, but from time to time they could change back into human form. In Scotland and in Ireland, the seal people were believed to have the power of changing into human form when they came onto land and shed their skins. If their skins were stolen from them, they could not return to the sea but had to live as humans. Many children were allegedly born out of unions between humans and seal folk, and the people of the Clan MacCodrum of the Outer Hebrides were said to have been descended from a seal-woman who married an islander. The Shetland and Orkney Isles are a particularly rich source of selkie legends. The story of the crofter and the seal-woman is of uncertain origin and has a number of slightly different versions. One version of the story comes from Shetland, another from Orkney. Other versions place the story on the Scottish mainland, or on other islands. As so often happens with tales of this sort, it has also blended with mermaid legend and very similar stories are told of a fisherman and a mermaid. Wherever the tale was first told, and whether it was first the story of mermaids or a seal folk, it has found a place in the imaginations of all those who have ever believed in these fabulous creatures.

assispattle and the stoorworm

Long ago in Norway, there lived a farmer and his wife. They had seven sons and a daughter. The youngest son was called Assispattle by his older brothers. He had another name, but they never used it. They called him Assispattle because he spent his evenings wallowing by the fire in the ashes and soot that lay around the fireplace, and his hair and clothes were always dirty, dusty and grey. He was badly treated by his family. All the dirtiest and meanest jobs in the house were given to him to do, and he was the butt of all his brothers' jokes. The only member of the family to show any kindness to Assispattle was his sister, who loved to listen to the wild and wonderful tales that he dreamt up in his head. But as soon as she was old enough, she was sent into service as a maid in the king's household, and Assispattle was left without a friend. When he tried to tell his brothers the stories that had come into his head, they cursed him for wasting their time, and beat him for lying. So Assispattle took to running wild round the countryside every day, telling his stories to the wind, and the dust from the ashes in his hair left a grey trail in the air behind him as he ran.

Far out in the waters of the sea around Norway there lived a great sea serpent, which was believed to be the most terrible creature of its kind. It was known as the Stoorworm. When it came upon the land, it could cause the most dreadful destruction, devouring crops and animals and whole chunks of the countryside in its massive jaws. And so it was a terrible day when news reached the king that the serpent was heading for his land. He knew that unless the serpent was stopped, his country would lie in ruins before long and his people would disappear forever. He called an emergency council to see what could be done, but there was not a man present who could think of a plan that might divert the beast from its course. Its poisonous breath could fell every living creature within miles. Its massive jaws could demolish the strongest of fortifications. There was no weapon that could be used against it. The council sat for three nights and three days and could still not come to a decision.

Then the queen drew her husband aside.

'It is useless to pit the mere strength of men against the Stoorworm,' she said to her husband. 'Its tongue alone is strong enough to sweep trees, roots and all, from the soil. It can demolish whole villages in one swift movement and sweep all the inhabitants into its mouth. No number of warriors can be great enough to compete against it. You must consult the sorcerer, to find some form of magic that will defeat the monster.'

The king agreed, with great reluctance. He thought the old sorcerer was deceitful and that his tricks were usless. But he could think of no better suggestion to make, and the great hulk of the Stoorworm was already visible, lying in wait in the icy blue-grey waters by the shore. He ordered the sorcerer to be brought before the council. The sorcerer was wizened and gnarled, with a long matted beard and wispy grey hair. 'This man before me does not look wise,' thought the king. 'He looks old, and worn, and useless.' But he asked for the sorcerer's advice none the less, and the sorcerer promised to have an answer by morning.

When the sorcerer came before the council the next day, his news was grim. The only way to keep the Stoorworm from devastating the land was to feed it with seven virgins every week. It was a terrible sacrifice for the people to make, but it was the only thing that might satisfy the monster's appetite until it decided to leave. If that failed, the sorcerer said, then they would be left with only one alternative and that was too terrible to think about. And so it was agreed that once a week, on a day designated by the king's council, seven virgins would be taken to the rocks by the shore and left to the mercies of the Stoorworm. The screams of the first seven sacrifices, as they waited for the tongue of the Stoorworm to sweep them into its mouth, almost tore the hearts out of those who could hear. And on the next appointed day, the cries of the second set of victims were even worse, for they had seen the fate of the first ones and knew what would happen. The people came from miles around to catch a glimpse of the dreadful beast as it devoured its prey, and the sight of it made the blood turn to ice in their veins. But high on the hillside, in the middle of the crowd, near to his brother, stood Assispattle, and he seemed strangely unafraid.

'I am not afraid of the monster,' he said to the wind. 'I would gladly take it on in combat, and I would win.'

Assispattle's brothers heard his careless words and punched and kicked him down the hillside back to their farm, calling him a lying braggart. But Assispattle let the blows rain down on him without complaint.

'I would fight you back, and beat you all,' he cried as they left him in a heap in the yard, 'but I have to save all my strength to do battle with the Stoorworm!'

Time passed and the people were growing desperate. How many more families would have to mourn the loss of their fairest maidens? Would the monster ever have had his fill? Every week they hoped that he would turn and leave, but every week, the snapping of his great jaws sent great waves crashing against the shore to tell them that his appetite was still unsatisfied. The people began to question the sorcerer's wisdom and asked the king to summon another council.

The council was gathered and the sorcerer summoned again. He seemed weaker, and more wizened than ever.

'Too many young women have died,' the king said to him, 'and yet the monster is as hungry as ever and we see no sign of him going. You told us there was an alternative. Tell us what it is, no matter how unthinkable it might be.'

The sorcerer raised himself up to his full height.

'If the monster is not satisfied with the fairest of citizens of this kingdom,' he said, 'then it is with great sorrow that I must declare that it has an appetite for more royal blood. The king's daughter must be given in sacrifice, or we will see our land devoured, acre by acre, by the Stoorworm.'

The king rose from his seat, tears in his eyes, and addressed the council.

'This is a cruel decision to ask me to make,' he said, 'for as anyone knows, there is no-one whom I hold more dear in all the world than my beautiful daughter. But I know that it is my duty as a king to do whatever must be done to save my kingdom and the lives of my people, and therefore, if this be the choice of the council, I give my consent for her to be fed to the monster.'

The men of the council could not raise their heads to look at their sorrowing king as one by one, they raised their hands in consent. All of them were silent, except one, an elderly noble who spoke out defiantly, with anger in his voice.

'If this is the will of the majority, I must go along with

it, but I beg to add one condition to our decision. This sorcerer has spoken before and on his advice, many fair maidens have perished to no avail. If we do as he says and sacrifice our princess, and the monster does not depart, then I want the sorcerer to be the next to die!'

His words were met with a roar of approval from the assembled company, and a date was set for the princess to be taken to meet her death.

The king had a few days left in which to try to save the princess. He sent messengers out to the farthest corners of the land, to find heroes who might be willing to try to repel the beast. As a reward, he promised the hand of his daughter in marriage to the man who succeeded. The princess was admired by every warm-blooded young man in the land, and it was not long before thirty-six young nobles came riding back to the palace, eager to accept the challenge. But none of them had laid eyes on the Stoorworm yet, and as soon as they did, two thirds of them quailed at first sight, and retreated. The remaining twelve took shelter in the palace, trying in vain to summon the courage to confront the beast a second time. The king gave them supper, but sat in the shadows and wept while they ate, for he knew that they would fail. It was the night before his daughter was due to be taken to the Stoorworm, and he could hear the splashes of the great waves that smashed into the shore as it snapped its jaws in anticipation.

Meanwhile, in the farmer's house some miles away, Assispattle sat among the ashes and wondered aloud, 'Why was I not asked to confront the Stoorworm? I am not afraid!' His brothers laughed contemptuously and kicked him again.

When the twelve remaining suitors had drunk their fill, they slunk off to bed. The old king sat on in the shadowy hall. Only Kemperlan, champion of all his warriors, remained to keep him company. At last the king rose from his chair, and went and lifted a great sword from the wall. It was the sword with which he had led his people to victory in battle countless times, when he was young and in his prime. But many years had passed since the king had last used it. He was now worn down with sorrow and care and had lost the vigour of his youth. Kemperlan at once understood what the king was thinking, but he could see all too plainly that the sword was too heavy for his master now.

'You cannot think of taking on the Stoorworm,' he said to the king. 'Why even I, the strongest of your warriors, dare not attempt it. I can see how your hands are stiff around the hilt of your sword, your grip is feeble and your wrists are cracking with the weight of it. You will not be able to raise it against the beast!'

But the king would brook no argument. He could not stand by and watch his daughter die. He would rather die in a fruitless struggle against the Stoorworm than live knowing he had done nothing to protect his own flesh and blood.

'You have been a loyal and devoted servant,' he told Kemperlan, 'and I could not have hoped for a better supporter than you. Now do this one thing, even if it is the last thing you ever do for me. Go down to the shore and prepare my boat. Then stay and guard her, at the ready. I shall come at first light.'

With a heavy heart, Kemperlan went to do the king's bidding, while his master closed his eyes and rested, preparing for the morning, when he faced certain death.

In the farmer's house, Assispattle woke from a restless doze and sat up. He could hear his mother and father whispering to each other in the corner of the room. They knew that the princess was due to meet her doom the next day, and like many other people who lived in the area, were making plans to travel down to the edge of the sea, where the monster lay sleeping, so that they could watch the spectacle.

'I will take you on my horse,' said the farmer, 'and we will get there before anyone else.'

The farmer's horse was the envy of all around, for when he instructed it, it could run faster than any other horse in the district. All the farmer's sons except Assispattle had ridden the horse, but it would only run its fastest for their father.

'If you really loved me,' the farmer's wife replied, 'then you would tell me how you get your horse to run so fast. Then I would be proud to sit in front of you on the saddle, wearing my finest clothes and with my hair tied up like a princess.'

The farmer hesitated, but his wife wheedled and cajoled and whispered loving words in his ear, and he gave in to her charms. Over in the fireplace, curled up in a pile of ashes, Assispattle kept his eyes tightly shut and listened.

'When I want my horse to pick up speed, I give him one gentle tap on his haunches with my foot,' said the farmer. He nudged her gently, making her laugh.

'Yes, yes,' she whispered, 'go on!'

'And when I want him to go faster, I give him two gentle

taps, just like this,' said the farmer, and he nudged her twice this time.

'I know, I know!' said his wife, 'but what do you do to make him run like the wind? That is what I really want to know!'

The farmer took a dried goose's windpipe from his pocket and showed it to his wife.

'I blow on this,' he said, 'and I hold on for dear life, for as soon as the horse hears it, he kicks up his heels and gallops, faster than the wildest winds of winter!'

Over by the fireplace, Assispattle heard his father's words, every one, and a great new story came into his head, which was better than any story he had ever told before. He waited until his father and mother were fast asleep, then he set about making the story come true.

Assispattle rose from the ashes. He took a pair of tongs and picked a smouldering peat from the edge of the fire and placed it in a large soup pot. Then he crept over to his sleeping parents. The goose's windpipe was lying at his father's side. Assispattle picked it up, and tiptoeing out of the house, went to the stable and saddled his father's horse. He tied the pot with the smouldering peat to the back of the saddle, then mounted the horse and tapped it gently on the haunch once with his right foot. The beast stood stock still. Assispattle tapped once with his left foot. The horse began to trot, out of the stable and into the yard. Then Assispattle tapped twice with his left foot, and the horse let out a whinny and began to canter. The farmer was woken by the sound of his horse's feet, and came running into the yard, but he was not quick enough. When he saw his youngest son disappearing into the distance with his precious horse, he let out a roar of fury and started to run. But Assispattle did not turn round. He lifted the goose's windpipe to his lips and blew into it, long and hard. The horse kicked up its heels and Assispattle clung on for dear life. They galloped off into the night at tremendous speed, leaving the farmer impotent with rage and disappointment.

Assispattle soon settled into the horse's rhythm. It ran swiftly, but smoothly. It was quick to respond to Assispattle's commands and at the slightest touch of the reins, it would change direction wherever he wanted it to go. It did not take them long to reach the shore. When they got there, Assispattle dismounted. He walked onto the narrow strip of sand beside the water and began to gather driftwood, heaping it into a great pile at the water's edge. Out on the water, he could see Kemperlan keeping vigil in the king's boat. The boat's sails were unfurled and at the ready, and its prow was pointing seawards, towards the rumbling, black island that was the sleeping monster's head. Assispattle set light to the pile of driftwood with the smouldering peat, then placed it back in its pot. He waited until the fire was blazing brightly, then he called out to Kemperlan.

'Come and warm yourself by the flames!' he cried. 'Why spend the night out there all alone in the cold and dark?'

Kemperlan watched the dancing flames of Assispattle's bonfire with envy, but he would not desert his post.

'This is the last thing I can do for my master the king,' he replied, 'and I will not disobey him and leave the vessel unguarded!'

'Very well,' said Assispattle, pretending that it did not matter. But Assispattle knew that every man has a weakness, and he suspected he might know what Kemperlan's weakness was.

He sat quietly for a moment or two, looking out to sea patiently. Then he rose, and took up a stick, poking gently at the sand around the bonfire. He scraped a few lines in the sand, then he poked at it again, looking as if he was doing nothing more than idling away the time and enjoying the warmth of the fire. After a few moments he stopped, then he poked the sand, and shouted, and poked the sand again, bending over and exclaiming, as if he had found something.

'Gold!' he cried out. 'Would you believe it! There is a pile of golden coins, right here, beneath the point of my stick!'

Within moments, Kemperlan turned the king's boat and was making for the shore. As soon as the boat reached shallow water, he jumped forward, dived from the prow onto the sand and began scraping the sand beside the fire. Assispattle did not waste a second. He took the pot with the smouldering peat and leapt on board the boat and raised the sails. Then taking the helm, he steered it back out to sea towards the Stoorworm's great head. Dawn was breaking as Assispattle drew close to the great hump in the water.

Back on shore, the king and a crowd of watchers were drawing near the water's edge. And when the king reached the beach, he did not find his faithful Kemperlan waiting for him in the boat. Instead, he found the greedy servant scraping a great hole in the sand with a stick, while the royal vessel headed out into deep water, with an ashen-haired stranger at the helm.

Assispattle manoeuvred the king's boat alongside the

Stoorworm's mouth. He remained determined and unafraid. He let down the sails and waited.

The sun came up, and the Stoorworm woke, opening its jaws in a great, wide, groaning yawn. The sea all around it surged and bubbled as it yawned. Gallons of water poured into the monster's mouth in waves, and Assipattle and the royal boat were swept along with the force of it. Into the monster's mouth sailed the boat with Assipattle in it, and everything all about him went dark. Assipattle clung to the side of the ship as it was tossed on the waves to the back of the monster's throat and right down its enormous, foul-smelling gullet. Down and down went boat, down to the entrance to the monster's stomach. The Stoorworm had many secrets hidden in there; all the things it had swallowed in the recent past swam in pieces in a murky sea of malodorous liquid, and the fat from all the creatures it had devoured lay in great greasy globules on the surface. When the boat reached the far side, Assipattle jumped out, taking his pot of smouldering peat with him, and began to hurry along the great passageway that led from the stomach, further into the entrails of the beast. Assipattle moved on through the dark recesses of the creature's gigantic innards, on and on through the stinking murk until he found where the liver was. He could smell the fat, and the monster's bile made the darkness glow eerily yellow. Assipattle stopped, and took the smouldering peat from its pot. He blew on it to bring the flames to life, then set it against a piece of fat by the Stoorworm's liver and blew again, until a bright orange glow told him that the fire had taken. Then he turned back and with all speed, headed back the way he had come.

The monster let out a deafening roar of pain as he felt the fire take hold in his liver, but Assispattle kept hurrying on. The stinking, slimy passageways inside the monster began to shudder and quake, but Assispattle kept his balance and did not stop. As fast as he might move, he could still feel the heat of the fire coming from behind him. Then just as Assispattle reached its stomach, the Stoorworm gave a great, heaving retch and vomited. A great wave of fluid poured out from its stomach, flooding the land along the shoreline. Assispattle was sucked into the stomach by the vacuum that was left behind. The monster belched, a terrible sound that sent the king and the people who had come to watch scurrying up the hillside in fear for their lives. Then it vomited again, and Assispattle was flung right out of its mouth, landing with a splash on the newly flooded ground at the water's edge. The king's boat floated in pieces beside him in the waters of the flood. Assispattle struggled onto dry land and made his way up the hillside to join the king and the other people, and they climbed onto the summit, out of harm's way, to watch the death throes of the Stoorworm.

The floods rose higher and higher as again and again the monster spewed out all the fluid from its cavernous insides. Then steam, issued forth, then smoke, great clouds of it, poured from the Stoorworm's mouth and nostrils, and the land and the water below the watchers was enveloped in a great grey cloud. The monster opened its mouth and screamed in pain and its great forked tongue shot out and curled skywards. The tongue was so long, it seemed as if it might stretch to the moon, and the great red forks of it disappeared into the highest clouds

of the sky and beyond. Then the monster let its tongue
fall down to the ground with a thundering crash. The
land beneath it shattered and divided, and the sea water
flowed in from both sides, making a passage between
the two segments of land. And that is how the sea came
to separate Denmark from Norway and Sweden. Then
the monster raised its head, higher than the clouds, and
shook it, once, twice, three times. All the teeth in its
head fell out with the force of the shaking, and scattered
in the seas all around. One set of teeth formed the
Orkney Isles, another formed Shetland and a third, the
Faroes. The monster's head fell back into the sea with an
almighty splash, and in its final agonies, the great beast
curled itself round and round into a coil. The body of
the dead Stoorworm formed Iceland, and the fires that
still smoulder deep within its belly heat the volcanoes
and bubbling springs that can be found there.

The king organised a great celebration in honour of
Assispattle's bravery, and offered the young hero the
hand of his precious daughter in marriage. Assispattle
had saved the princess's life, after all, and had spared
the whole of the land from a terrible fate. And so it was
that Assispattle moved from his place among the ashes to
the royal palace and began a new life of happiness with
his beautiful bride. He was reunited with his sister, who
became chief lady-in-waiting to the young royal couple,
and now that he was at a distance from his cruel brothers,
who had become considerably more humble since the day
of the great deed, Assispattle forgave them. At a special
meeting of the king's council, a vote was passed to send
the sorcerer into exile, and from then on, the king paid
no heed to his foolish wife's advice.

As the years passed, Assipattle grew in stature and turned into a handsome hero, unrecognisable as the scrawny, ash-smeared lad he had once been. He still loved to invent stories, and in his wife he found an eager audience. As the two of them lay in bed together at night, the princess would lean her head on Assipattle's shoulder and listen to his soft voice bring the monsters, giants and heroic deeds in his imagination to life. He had found happiness at last, and it was well deserved. And when the old king eventually passed away peacefully in his sleep one summer's morning, the people of his kingdom could not think of a better man to succeed him than brave, noble Assipattle.

the crofter and the seal-woman

There was once a young crofter who had a patch of land by the sea, where he eked out a meagre living, growing a few basic food crops. He had a small boat and used this to supplement his income, setting crab and lobster pots on the seabed along the shoreline when the weather permitted, and selling his catch locally.

One evening, as the crofter was walking by the shore towards the cove where he kept his boat tied up on the beach, he heard the sound of women's laughter coming from behind a rocky outcrop close to the water's edge. The crofter moved closer, his instincts telling him he should not make a sound that might disturb the revellers. He peered over the top of the rocks and saw a group of beautiful women with long, silken hair, dancing on a small stretch of sand at the water's edge. The crofter suspected at once that these must be seal-women, and, sure enough, his suspicions were confirmed when he saw that laid out on the rocks behind the dancing figures, were the magical skins which they had shed when they came ashore.

The sun began to go down, but the women danced on, unaware of their silent watcher. The crofter was transfixed. There was one among them who had caught his eye, and he could not take his gaze from her. Her eyes were as black as night and her hair fell about her shoulders in a shimmering curtain of gold. Her skin glowed, an opalescent white tinged with pink by the rosy light of sunset. She was the most beautiful thing he had ever seen.

The tide was coming in and bit by bit, the water was creeping further up the sand. The seal-women stopped dancing and moved towards the rocks, ready to gather up their skins and return to the sea. Last to come was the one who had stolen the heart of the crofter. One by one, the beautiful creatures grasped their skins and slipped them onto their bodies, pulling the silver-grey cowls over their heads. But just as the last one was reaching out for hers, the crofter jumped from his hiding place and took a hold of it. He could not bear to see her change back into a seal and disappear. When the seal-woman's companions saw what had happened, they knew they could do nothing to help her. With a cry of despair, they slipped back into the sea and disappeared. A few moments later, the head of a bull seal broke the surface. The poor creature stared helplessly towards shore, with anguish in its eyes. It was the husband of the seal-woman.

The seal-woman begged the crofter to give her back her skin, and let her return to her home and her family, but the crofter's passion made him selfish. He could not bring himself to do as she wished. He asked her to become his wife. He swore that he would make her happy in a new life with him on land and that he would care for her as long as he lived. The seal-woman was trapped. She had no choice but to agree, and so the crofter led her back to his cottage. He tried to soothe her with kind words and promises, but still he could not set her free, and clutched the sealskin tight against his chest to keep it safe from her. He waited until late at night when she had finally fallen asleep, then he took the skin and wrapped it carefully in blankets. He placed the bundle in a wooden box, and hid it in beneath some straw in the darkest corner of the byre, where he knew she would never find it.

Years passed. The crofter was blissfully happy with his beautiful wife. They had seven healthy children and life was good. The crofter worked hard to support his family, and although they were not rich, they had everything they needed. The seal-woman was a good wife and mother, and turned the crofter's house into a warm and loving home. The crofter loved her more than he could ever say, and she, for her part, was very fond of him, but in spite of all her husband's kindness and the great love she had for her children, she could never forget the place she had come from. She had once been completely happy, and nothing that the crofter could say or do would ever compensate her for her loss. Sometimes, late at night, when the family was asleep, she slipped away from the cottage and tiptoed to the water's edge. She would stand there for most of the night, staring out to sea, remembering her lost kinfolk and hoping for a glimpse of their heads bobbing up and down in the moonlit waters. Somewhere out there, waiting for her, was her first husband, a selkie just like she, and her heart was still with him.

One day, when the crofter was out working in the fields, the seal-woman was in the cottage preparing food when the youngest child came running in, carrying something in his arms. He had found the wooden box that had been hidden so long ago in the corner of the byre. With a child's natural curiosity, he had opened it and discovered the sealskin concealed inside. The boy knew nothing about his mother's past. He only wanted to ask her what it was he had found, that felt so soft and warm, and had the fresh, salty smell of the sea in its silvery hairs. The seal-woman gently took it from him, her eyes filling with tears.

When the crofter came home that night, the cottage was strangely quiet. The children were all fast asleep in their beds, and a pot of soup bubbled gently on the fire, but his wife was not there to greet him, and there was nothing to indicate where she might have gone. A sudden fear gripped the crofter's heart and he ran out to the byre. When he found the wooden box open and its contents gone, he thought his heart would break. The seal-woman had gone back to her own folk, and to the husband she had before him.

In time the crofter found another wife, a good, kind woman who loved him dearly and cared for his children as if they were her own. He was content with his lot. But sometimes, late at night, just as the seal-woman had done before him, he would slip away on his own and stand at the water's edge, staring out to sea, straining his eyes for one last glimpse of his first and only true love.

the seaL hunter's Lesson

This story comes from the far north of the Scottish mainland, near John o' Groats.

There was once a man who lived on the coast and made his living from hunting seals. Seal hunting could be quite a lucrative profession. There was good money to be made from the sealskins, and from the blubber which could be burned in oil lamps. The seal-hunter did not think that what he did was cruel. It was what he did to earn his keep. You could not afford to be sentimental about it. You avoided looking into the creatures' eyes and you closed your ears to their cries of pain. You went for a quick, clean kill, which was kindest to the animal and kept the skin intact. You could not let yourself think about the life you were taking.

One dark night the seal-hunter had already gone to bed when he heard a hammering on his door. Muttering under his breath at the inconvenience of being disturbed at such a late hour, he stumbled across to the door and opened it to find a stranger on the threshold. The stranger made no apology for interrupting the seal hunter's sleep. Instead, he told him that his master wished to see him to discuss some important business, and told him to get dressed and come with him right there and then. Something in the stranger's tone of voice warned the seal hunter that it was not wise to argue. Besides, business was business, and he might find that the effort was well worth it. He pulled on some clothes and followed his visitor out into the night. A black stallion was waiting outside, pawing impatiently at the ground with its hooves. The stranger leapt into the saddle and beckoned the seal hunter to climb up behind him. The hunter had no time to settle himself comfortably on the horse's back, for as soon as his leg was over the saddle, the horse took off like the wind. How far they travelled, the hunter could not tell, for the sky was overcast and there was no moon to light their way. But of one thing he could be sure. He was travelling faster that he had ever thought it possible to go on a horse. Were it not for the fact that he could feel the thud of the horse's feet pounding the ground beneath them, he might have been convinced that they were flying.

At last the stranger pulled on the reins and brought the horse to a standstill. The two men dismounted. The sound of waves crashing on rocks far below then told the hunter that they were high above the sea. Peering into the darkness ahead, he could just make out the edge of the cliff, a few feet away. There was no sign of a house anywhere around, and the hunter was becoming increasingly apprehensive. Why had the stranger brought him here? Where was the man whom they were supposed to be meeting? He turned to the stranger to ask, but the words were hardly out of his mouth when the stranger suddenly took hold of him, clasping his arms to his sides in a vice-like grip. All his breath seemed to leave his body as he was swept off his feet. The stranger kept a hold of him as they both careered over the edge of the cliff and plunged towards the waves below. Everything went black.

The next thing the hunter knew was that he was far beneath the waves, on the sea bed. The stranger had disappeared, and in his place was a large, dark bull seal. The seal beckoned to him and led him over to a door, opening it and signalling for him to enter. The hunter found himself in a place such as he could never have imagined. It was a great hallway, from which corridors led to a series of smaller chambers. All around him were seals, young old, male and female, weeping and groaning. The hunter was perplexed and frightened. What was the cause of the creatures' distress? And how could he, a human being, be in such a place when there was no air for him to breathe? Then he looked down at himself and realised that he had changed. His clothes were gone, and his body no longer bore any resemblance to that of a man. He had become a seal. His heart was filled with a terrible fear, as he allowed himself to be led out of the hall and into one of the chambers. There, surrounded by grieving attendants, lay a large bull seal. It was bleeding heavily from a gaping wound in its belly and its life was ebbing away. The hunter's guide picked up something from beside the wounded seal and handed it to him. It was a hunting knife, its blade smeared in blood. The hunter recognised it at once as his own. He had lost it that morning. He had plunged it into a seal, but the blow had missed the mark and although the seal had been injured, it had struggled free, sliding into the water and away, with the knife still stuck in its flesh. The dying creature before him must be that very same seal! Now the hunter became almost hysterical with fear. What terrible revenge had his captors planned for him?

His guide put the knife back down and turned to the hunter.

'You are responsible for what has happened, so you must make it better,' he said. 'Place your hands upon the wound and close it to undo the harm that you have done.'

The hunter did as he was told. He placed his hands either side of the gaping wound in the seal's belly. The edges of the wound moved together, and the bleeding stopped. When the hunter removed his hands, the wound had healed completely and his victim was already visibly regaining strength.

The hunter waited in dread to see what would happen next. At length, the seal that he had wounded lifted its head and began to speak.

'We do not need to keep you here, and it is not right for you to be away from your own kind,' he said. 'We would like to return you to our own home. But we must have one promise from you in return. If you swear that you will never harm another seal as long as you live, we will take you right back to your own doorstep and compensate you for your loss of livelihood. If you cannot promise us what we ask, then we cannot let you return.'

The hunter longed for the familiar surroundings of his own four walls. He had not been away for long, but he ached to feel the wind on his face, to see the sky above him and to feel dry land beneath his feet. He gave his word without hesitation. The assembled group nodded their heads in silent farewell and the same seal that had guided him into the seals' kingdom led the hunter out through the door again. For the second time, he felt his body being gripped with great force. Then he was moving up through the water at great speed. Within moments he was standing at the top of the cliff beside the stranger. He felt his lungs swell with the cold, clean air, and he let out a great sigh of relief. He was a man again. The black stallion was waiting for them, just where they had left him. This time the hunter needed no encouragement to climb up behind his companion. He jumped onto the horse's back and they set off on the homeward journey at lightning speed.

Dawn was breaking as the stranger let the hunter down on his own doorstep once more. The hunter was silent, shaken to the core by all that had happened. The stranger turned the horse, ready to leave, then leant down and pressed a leather pouch into the hunter's hand. Seconds later, he was gone, and the sound of his horse's feet was fading far into the distance. With shaking hands, the hunter opened the leather pouch and emptied out its contents onto the ground in front of him. A pile of gold coins glistened at his feet. He need never work again.

the seaL of suLe skerry

The following tale is based on a ballad, which comes from Orkney.

A young woman sat weeping with her baby in her arms. She rocked the child gently to and fro, and sobbed her sad story to anyone who would listen. She wept because she did not know who the father of her baby was, or where he might be. He had left her to bring her child up alone. She did not know it, but the man who had fathered her child was a selkie, and he had gone back to the sea.

One day as she sat cradling her child and weeping softly, a seal appeared beside her.

'I am the father of your child,' he said, 'and I cannot marry you. I will see that he is provided for. But when the child is seven years old I will come to take him back where he belongs, with me.' The seal dropped a leather pouch of money beside the woman and child, and disappeared back into the sea.

And so the young woman nursed the child from babyhood into boyhood alone. The child was strong, healthy and happy, but she knew that with every passing day, she had a little less time left with him.

At last the dreaded day came, when the boy was little more than seven years old. Mother and son were down by the shore together when the seal appeared again, and beckoned the woman to come to him.

'The time has come for me to claim my son,' said the seal. 'Take this as your payment for caring for him.' He placed another pouch of gold in the woman's hands. He turned to the child, and placed a golden chain around the boy's neck. 'If you are down by the shore and see some seals out on the skerry,' said the seal, 'look for one that has a golden chain. That will be a sign to you that your child is safe.'

The seal drew the child towards him and moved to the water's edge.

'But what of me?' said the woman, her eyes filling with tears. 'I have no husband, and soon I will have no son. What will I do?'

'You will find another one to love,' said the seal. 'A good man will come, a soldier, and you will spend many happy years with him. But there will come a morning in May when your husband will go down to the shore and shoot two seals. One will be your son, and the other one will be me.'

There was no time for more questions. The seal signalled to the boy and the two of them, father and son, dived into the water together and disappeared.

Years passed. The young woman did find another man to

love, and as it turned out, he was a soldier. He was a loving and loyal husband and although the woman never forgot the seal, or her precious son, she did find happiness with her new partner. Then one day her husband went out with his gun, and when he returned, he told her that he had shot two seals. One of the seals had had a golden chain around his neck. When her husband showed her the chain, the woman was broken-hearted. She realised that the last words the seal had said to her had finally come true, and that he and her dear son were the ones who had been killed by her husband.

the mermaid's revenge

There are almost as many Scottish stories told about merfolk as there are about selkies, for people were equally fascinated with these creatures that were half human and half fish. Mermen and mermaids were believed to be able to shed their fish tails when they came onto dry land, just as selkies could shed their skins.

But while the stories of the selkie people almost exclusively conjure up an image of a gentle creature which could be surprisingly forgiving to man in spite of his cruelty, some of the tales of the mer-people show mermaids in a less kindly light. A mermaid could make a man fall in love with her, but she could also lure him to his death. And woe betide the human who crossed a mermaid, as the following story illustrates.

There was once a merchant who lived by the sea, in a grand house overlooking a sandy cove. At the edge of the cove there was a large, black rock. This rock had been worn so smooth by the waves that its surface gleamed, and the top of it was so comfortably rounded that it looked just like a plump, well-feathered cushion. It was the favourite seat of a mermaid. Every night she came to the cove and sat upon the rock, stretching out her tail over the polished stone so that it shimmered in the moonlight. Then she began to sing. The merchant and his wife were sound sleepers and although they heard the eerie sound of the mermaid's singing from time to time, it did not disturb them unduly. They were used to it. But when the merchant's wife gave birth to her first child, everything changed.

The baby seemed contented enough during the day, but every night, after darkness had fallen, he would grow fretful and begin to cry. Once he started, nothing would console him, and the nursemaid who cared for him became exhausted with the effort of trying to soothe his tears. The baby's crying disturbed his mother as well, preventing her from sleeping. She took turns with the nursemaid, walking up and down the nursery floor with her son in her arms as she tried in vain to rock him to sleep. One night as she was doing this, the child paused in his crying to draw breath for a few seconds. There was silence in the nursery, but outside, the merchant's wife could hear the sound of the mermaid singing in the darkness, and she realised that it was the singing that was upsetting her son. It was only at night that the child cried, and it was only at night that the mermaid sang.

The next night, a servant from the house was sent to speak to the mermaid, to ask her to stop her singing, or to move away. The request was politely made, but rudely refused. There was a note of defiance in the songs that the mermaid sang that night, and the sound could be clearly heard in every room of the merchant's house. And so it went on. Several times, the mermaid was begged to stop her singing, but every time she was approached, her response was to sing all the louder. And the louder she sang, the louder the baby cried.

The merchant's wife reached the end of her tether. She called her male servants together and told them to go down to the shore with hammers and pickaxes, to smash the mermaid's rock to pieces. The men did as she had asked, and by the end of the day, there was nothing left of the rock but a heap of small, black, jagged stones. Now, perhaps, the mermaid would accept defeat gracefully and find another place to sing her strange songs.

But when the mermaid reached shore that evening and saw what had been done, not a thought of defeat crossed her mind. She was beside herself with rage that her beautiful singing stone had been destroyed, and she was determined to get her revenge. She lifted her voice to a pitch that it had never reached before, and screamed out a curse that was carried by the wind coming in from the sea, right to the ears of the merchant's wife. The mermaid's words struck horror into the hearts of all those who heard them. The venom and strength in her tone were terrible to hear, as she shrieked that tragedy would descend upon the household, and that the merchant's family line would die out. Upstairs in the nursery, the force of the sound began to rock the baby's cradle back and forth, back and forth, with increasing violence. When mermaid's last, terrible song was over, the merchant's wife hurried upstairs to attend to her child. She found him lying dead beneath his upturned cradle. Just as the mermaid had predicted, there were no more children, and the merchant died without an heir to succeed him.

two taLes of the bLue meN

When the tide is turning and the wind is fast asleep,
And not a wave is curling on the wide, blue, deep,
Oh, the waters will be churning in the stream that never
    smiles,
Where the Blue Men are splashing round the Shiant Isles!

As the summer wind goes droning o'er the sun-bright seas,
And the Minch is all a-dazzle to the Hebrides,
They will skim along like salmon—you can see their
    shoulders gleam,
And the flashing of their fingers in the Blue Men's stream.

But when the blast is raving and the wild tide races,
The Blue Men are breast-high with foam-grey faces;
They'll plunge along with fury while they sweep the spray
    behind,
Oh, they'll bellow o'er the billows and wail upon the
    wind!

And if my boat be storm-tossed and beating for the bay,
They'll be howling and be growling as they drench it with
    their spray;—
For they'd like to heel it over to their laughter when it
    lists,
Or crack the keel behind them, or stave it with their fists.

Oh, weary on the Blue Men, their anger and their wiles!
The whole day long, the whole night long, they're
	splashing round the isles;
They'll follow every fisher—ah! They'll haunt the fisher's
	dream—
When billows toss, oh! Who would cross the Blue Men's
	stream!

Donald A. Mackenzie

Selkies and mermaids were said to dwell in many places
around the coast of Scotland, but the Blue Men are a
phenomenon to be found in only one place. Between the
Island of Lewis and the Shiant Isles lies a narrow strait, part
of the Minch, which is known in Gaelic as Sruth nam Fear
Gorm – The Stream of the Blue Men. Even when the seas
all around are calm, the water in the Stream of the Blue
Men can be rough and treacherous, and even today many
skippers choose to steer clear of the strait and take a more
circuitous route, for fear of the Blue Men. Anyone who
has been at sea when the weather is wild, or has seen the
force with which white-capped waves, several feet high,
come crashing in to shore when a storm is blowing, can
imagine how it is possible that sailors, caught in the teeth
of a storm, might conjure up in their minds a picture of
raging, white-haired blue figures attacking their boat. But
if the Blue Men are no more than mental images which
spring to into the heads of seamen in storm-tossed ships,
then why are there no Blue Men anywhere else in the
waters around Scotland, or even around the world?

The Blue Men were said to live in underwater caves in
the Minch, and to occupy themselves by churning up the

waters in the strait by the Shiant Isles. Sometimes they slept, and it was only then that the waters in the strait settled down to peace for a brief spell. As soon as the Blue Men awoke, the waves would rise. The Blue Men would stir the waters with their long arms, scattering spray and foam all around. They took particular pleasure in attacking boats. They posted sentinels at the entrance to the strait and when a boat approached, the sentinels would signal to their companions lying in wait under the water, who would then come to the surface to stir up trouble. They would thrust their heads and chests out of the water and frighten the watching sailors. They would hurl abuse at the skipper, and jostle and shove the vessels to make them turn over, or pull on the rudder to force a ship off course and onto the rocks. Some folk referred to the strait as The Current of Destruction, and with good reason. Several boats were wrecked in the waters of the strait, and many times the blame for the disaster was placed upon the malicious activities of the Blue Men.

It was said that one way to outwit the Blue Men was to develop a skill in composing rhyming couplets, and the following tale illustrates this belief.

The Blue Men were lying dozing beneath the waves when the sentinels gave warning that a large ship was approaching. They swam to the surface in their hordes. They could see the great white sails of the vessel in the distance. It was a big ship, and they would have their work cut out for them if they were to capsize this one. The ship moved into the strait and several of the Blue Men dived below the surface and pulled on the keel, but the vessel moved on, sure and steady, and their efforts were to no avail. Others swarmed along the sides of the ship, thumping it with their fists, but the ship was built of the strongest, thickest timbers and they could not punch a hole in it. Nor could they move the rudder. The ship stayed right on course, steering a safe path through the strait. The chief of the Blue Men rose up out of the waves in fury. As he had done so often before with other ships, he challenged the skipper to a battle in verse.

'Man of the black cap, what do you say
As your proud ship cleaves the brine?'

The skipper did not hesitate to reply.

'My speedy ship takes the shortest way
And I'll follow you line by line.'

The chief of the Blue Men continued the challenge.

'My men are eager, my men are ready
To drag you beneath the waves!'

But the skipper was undaunted. His response came back, quick as a flash.

'My ship is speedy, my ship is steady;
If it sank it would wreck your caves.'

The chief of the Blue Men knew he had been beaten. No skipper had ever been able to answer his challenges so quickly and so cleverly. He could have no power over such a skipper, or his ship. Reluctantly, he signalled to his men and they sank below the waves. The ship sailed on through the strait unharmed, its tall mast straight and true and its snow-white sails puffed out with pride.

This story tells how people discovered that the Blue Men had names.

In summer, when the weather was fine, the Blue Men sometimes took their rest on the surface of the sea. On one occasion, a fishing boat stole into the strait undetected by the Blue Men, and the fishermen spied one of them sleeping, his head pillowed by the waves. The fishermen reached over the side of the boat, and gently, so as not to wake him, they pulled him on board. They laid him on the deck and bound him with as many ropes as they could find, determined that even if he struggled with all his might, he would not be able to escape.

But the capture of the Blue Man had not gone unnoticed. The waters around the fishing boat began to churn, and the fishermen turned to see that two of their captive's companions were coming after them to rescue their comrade. As they ploughed through the waves, the Blue Men called out to volunteer their help to the captive.

'Duncan will be one man,' called the first.

'Farquhar will be two!' called the second one.

The sound of their voices woke the sleeping Blue Man and he jumped up, snapping the ropes that bound him as if they were thin strands of thread.

'Ian Mhor has no need of help!' he called. And with that, he disappeared over the edge of the boat, leaving the surprised fishermen with nothing but a tangle of frayed rope on the deck in front of them.

Legendary Places

the Gold of Largo Law

Largo Law is a small volcanic hill in Fife, overlooking the town of Lower Largo on the Forth Estuary. It was believed at one time that the hill had been created when the Devil dropped a boulder on it, and at the top of it there is an outcrop of stone known as the Devil's Chair.

For hundreds of years, it has been said that somewhere deep within the hill is a store of hidden gold, or a gold mine, and although no-one has found a trace of it, legend has it that there was once a shepherd who came tantalisingly close to discovering the treasure.

The shepherd came from Balmain, and he grazed his sheep on the north side of the hill. It was common knowledge that the hill was haunted by a grim spectre. People said that the spectre had a great secret, and that it would pass it on to anyone that was brave enough to approach it and ask, but no-one had dared, not even the shepherd.

Then the shepherd's curiosity finally became strong enough to overcome his fear. He was making his way down from the hill one evening after dark when he sensed the familiar ghostly presence nearby. With his heart in his mouth, he spoke to the spectre and asked what it was that kept it prowling around Largo Law every night when all good folk were fast asleep. The ghost told the shepherd that if he returned to the hill the next night at an appointed time, it would tell him where hidden gold was to be found. However, there were two conditions to be fulfilled before the spectre could keep its end of the bargain. The conditions were put before the shepherd as follows:

If Auchindowie cock disnae craw,
And Balmain horn disnae blaw,
I'll tell ye where the gowd mine is in Largo Law.

The shepherd wasted not a moment. He went straight down the hill and personally saw to it that all the cockerels in Auchindowie, or within earshot of Largo Law, were slaughtered. Having done that, he went to Tammie Norrie, the cowherd of Balmain, and told him very firmly not to blow his horn at any time the following evening. The next night, satisfied that things would go smoothly, the shepherd set off up Largo Law, ready to find out the great secret. He waited for a few moments and then, exactly at the agreed time, the spectre appeared in front of him. The shepherd waited with baited breath for the secret to be revealed, but just as the spectre was about to divulge the location of the gold mine, the unmistakable sound of a cow horn could be heard in the distance. It was Tammie Norrie. Whether by accident or by design, he had ignored the shepherd's instructions. The shepherd stared, wide-eyed with dismay, as the spectre vanished into nothing, and its voice boomed out from the darkness:

Woe to the man that blew the horn,
For out of the spot he shall ne'er be borne.

Poor Tammie Norrie fell dead where he had been standing. When his body was found, and the locals tried to take it away, they found that it was stuck firmly to the spot. They were forced to leave his corpse where it had fallen. In place of a burial, they built a cairn of stones over him. The place came to be known as Norrie's Law.

The gold mine on Largo Law was never discovered. But there is an interesting sequel to the legend. In 1819, a tinker made a surprising discovery on Norrie's Law. He unearthed a stone coffin, containing a suit of armour and some items of silver. Although most of his find is thought to have been melted down, some items have been preserved in the Museum of Antiquities in Edinburgh. It was not gold, certainly, but it was treasure of a sort, and possibly the only precious secret that Largo Law is ever likely to yield.

the chatter of the birds: how eilean donan was built

Eilean Donan Castle is among the best known and best loved of Scottish castles. It stands on an islet at the place where Loch Alsh meets Loch Duich and Loch Long. Its picture-perfect setting has assured its photograph a place in numerous calendars, photography books and Scottish tourist guides that are marketed internationally. Consequently, the image of the castle has become, for many potential visitors to Scotland, the image of Scotland. There is evidence of a Pictish settlement at the site of Eilean Donan, but the first castle was established in the early thirteenth century, during the reign of Alexander II (1214–1250), and served as a stronghold against attacks from Norway. The Macraes became Constables of the Castle in 1509 and defended the castle successfully against attack and siege for two hundred years. Then in 1719, there was a Jacobite rising in support of James VII, the Old Pretender, and Spanish supporters of the Jacobite cause were quartered in Eilean Donan. A small English fleet was dispatched to attack the castle. The Spaniards, outnumbered and outclassed by the English troops and artillery, surrendered, and the castle was left in ruins. The building as it stands today dates from the early twentieth century, the result of a loving restoration of the castle carried out between 1912 and 1932 by Lieutenant Colonel John Macrae-Gilstrap.

The following legend about how the castle of Eilean Donan first came to be built adds a mystical aspect to its many charms.

A chief, who lived in Kintail became the proud father of a son. The chief was a man who suffered from an inflated sense of his own importance and placed himself on a pedestal high above the lower classes, dismissing them as superstitious fools. He had heard of an ancient belief that if a child were to be given its first drink from the skull of a raven, it would develop powers that no ordinary human possessed.

More for his own amusement than anything else, the chief decided to use his own child to put the superstition to the test, confident that he would disprove it. As soon the child was ready to be weaned from the breast, the chief provided the nursemaid with a raven's skull, and ordered that he be given his first drink out of it. Once the child had taken his first sip from the skull, he became able to understand the language of the birds, and to converse with them. This did not immediately become evident to the chief, for the child was still a baby. When at last the chief realised that his son could talk to the birds, he was most taken aback, but his disappointment at the failure of his experiment was fortunately outweighed by the amusement he derived from the boy's extraordinary ability. His amusement, however, would be short-lived.

The boy grew into adulthood, and his relationship with his vain father was reasonably amicable. Then one day the chief asked his son to tell him why the starlings had set up such a chatter around the house, and what they were saying. His son replied that the starlings were talking about a day to come, when the chief would wait upon his son at table. The pompous chief was so incensed by this insult that he banished his son from the family home and lands.

Forced by his father to embark upon a wandering life, the chief's son travelled many miles, and finally sailed to France. When he got there, he learned that the peace of the king's palace was disrupted by a great flock of sparrows, which made a continual noise, almost deafening in volume, all around the royal apartments. The young man made his way to the palace and offered his services to the king, knowing that he could communicate with the troublesome birds. It did not take him long to discover that a great feud had blown up between the birds, and the noise that disturbed the king so much was one of perpetual arguments in which none was willing to concede defeat. The chief's son made time to speak with all of the winged warriors and finally negotiated a peace that restored their angry screeches to a contented chirruping which did not offend the ear of the king. The king was greatly impressed and rewarded the chief's son with a ship, and a full crew to sail it, so that he could continue his wanderings by sea.

The chief's son sailed from country to country, filling his eyes and ears with strange sights and sounds, his mind feasting on new experiences almost daily. Everywhere he went, his talent for conversing with the birds caused wonderment, and his fame spread through many lands. He collected gifts of all kinds from the places that he visited, and he kept them as souvenirs. Soon his ship was laden with exotic goods.

After some years, the ship came to a distant land whose name is not known. When he disembarked at the port, the chief's son learned that the king of the country was greatly troubled by a plague of rats, that infested the palace and the grounds, and could not be got rid of. There was nothing that the chief's son could ask the birds to do in such a situation, but he knew he had the solution to the king's problem on board his ship. He had a cat, an agile and cunning hunter, which had an insatiable appetite for the chase. He gave the cat to the king, and soon the numbers of rats scurrying around the royal palace began to dwindle. The king was delighted to see the problem so quickly and simply brought under control, and asked the chief's son if he might keep the cat. The chief's son agreed, and was rewarded with a great casket of gold.

The chief's son had by now seen enough of the world and longed for sight of his own country once again. He set a course for Scotland and some weeks later his ship, with its cargo of riches, sailed into Loch Alsh. The sight of such a grand vessel set up quite a stir in the district. Anxious to create a good impression on what seemed to be a visitor of great importance, the vain old chief was the first to offer hospitality to the captain and crew. And so it came to pass that the chief's son and his men were taken to the chief's home, and provided with the finest food and drink that could be found. And, as the starlings had prophesied so many years before, the chief served his own son at table. When the traveller revealed his true identity to his father, the old man was almost struck dumb with shock.

The chief's son had learned a great deal in the years that he had been away, and his knowledge of the world was unsurpassed. He had also grown in wisdom and stature, and soon became recognised throughout the land as a great man. And it is said that it was in recognition of his wisdom and greatness that King Alexander gave the chief's son the honour of being the one to oversee the building of the castle at Eilean Donan, to defend Kintail and the lands beyond from Norse attack.

the Legend of corryvreckan

The Waterpool of Corryvreckan is situated in the gulf of the same name, a narrow stretch of water separating the island of Jura, to the south, from Scarba, to the north. Although the waters can seem quite calm at times, when the tides are right the whirlpool can be an awesome sight. It is here, according to ancient belief, that the Cailleach Beur, the winter goddess figure, washed her clothes in the swirling waters. The legend from which Corryvreckan gets its name is a sad one.

There was once a young prince named Breackan, a son of a king of Lochlin, who fell head over heels in love with a princess of the isles. The princess's father wanted his daughter to have a husband of great courage, and would only consent to give her away in marriage to the prince if he successfully completed a challenge that was set for him. He was to anchor his boat in the whirlpool and stay there for three days and three nights. Only if he survived this could he claim the hand of the princess. The young prince returned to Norway to prepare for the task. He had three ropes made with which to tie his little boat to its anchor. The first rope was made from sheep's wool, and the second from hemp. The third rope was more special than the first two, for it was woven from the hair of innocent maidens. The prince believed that this rope, strengthened by the virtue of the maidens whose hair had been used to make it, would be the one that would save him. He sailed back to Jura, taking his faithful dog along with him for company, and anchored his boat in the middle of the whirlpool. On the first day, the waters on the whirlpool bubbled and swirled, and by nightfall, the rope made of wool had snapped. One the second day, the boat was tossed and tugged here and there for hour after hour until finally, the rope of hemp was torn in two. Now the boat had only one rope to secure it to its anchorage. But the prince kept faith that the maidens' hair would hold strong and so he faced the third day with unwavering courage. On the third day, the whirlpool was wilder than ever, but the hours passed, and still the boat stayed tied to its anchor, in spite of all the tugging and heaving of the waves. The prince thought that his challenge would be successful, for there were not many minutes to go before his three days were up. But the rope that held his boat had a flaw. One of the maidens who had given her hair to make it was not as innocent as she had claimed. The strands of her hair weakened the rope, and just as the challenge was almost complete, the rope frayed and snapped. The prince's boat was sucked into the swirling vortex of water. The prince was drowned, but his faithful dog battled against the currents and survived. It struggled ashore onto the island, dragging its master's body with it. The unlucky prince was buried in a cave, which was named after him.

smoo cave

Smoo Cave, in Durness, is a large three-chambered limestone cave, situated on the coast, just above high tide level. The first chamber is easily accessible, but the second less so as a stream, the Alt Smoo, flows through a hole in the roof of the cave as a waterfall, landing in a deep pool below. The cave is associated with a number of legends. It was commonly believed in times gone by that hillsides and caves contained hidden entrances to the world of the Sidhe, or the fairy realm. Smoo cave is only one of several around Scotland that are associated with a legend that relates to this belief: that of a disappearing piper.

The story is that the piper marches into the cave, playing his pipes, and no trace of him is ever seen again, although sometimes the sound of his playing can be heard very faintly, as if coming from somewhere far within the earth. Smoo is also associated with a legend that bears some similarities to the story of the Murder Hole, which is also told in this book. According to the legend, there was a highwayman who plagued the district in the seventeenth century. His name was McMurdo, and he was a murderous villain. Not content with robbing his hapless victims, he took their lives as well, killing them by dropping them through the hole made by the stream into the cave, some eighty feet below.

The most well-known legends relating to Smoo Cave concern the notorious Wizard of Reay, Donald Mackay. He was in reality quite a fearsome character by all accounts, and consequently a number of legends developed around him. It was said that the Wizard of Reay had studied the black arts in Italy, under the skilled tuition of the Devil himself. According to tradition, when his studies were completed the Wizard of Reay got up to leave with the other students. He was last in line to go, and the Devil, as was customary, tried to steal him as his own. But Reay was wise to the Devil's tricks. Calling out 'The De'il take the hindmost!' he made a bolt for it, leaving the Devil with only his shadow. From that day on, it was said, the Wizard of Reay was without a shadow. It was also said that Reay used to chain his enemies to an iron ring set into the stone by the entrance to Smoo Cave, and leave them to drown in the waters of the incoming tide.

There are two stories about encounters between the Wizard of Reay and the Devil in Smoo Cave. The first tells how Reay was out with his dog in the middle of the night and entered the cave. He was still in the first chamber when his dog ran ahead into the second. Shortly after the dog disappeared, Reay heard it give a terrible howl, and seconds later it was back in the first chamber, frightened half to death and without a hair on its body. Reay realised that the Devil must be close at hand, and guessed that a trap had been set for him, so that the Devil could claim the soul he had been deprived of before. Reay was saved in the nick of time by the dawn. The first rays of the morning sun streamed into the cave and the Devil fled, blasting a hole in the roof to escape. A slightly different version of the same legend has the Devil accompanied by two witches, providing an explanation for the three holes is the cave roof.

According to the second legend, when Reay was deep inside Smoo Cave one day he came upon a small wooden casket. Curious to find out what was inside, Reay poked a hole in the casket, and out popped a little man, not more than a couple of inches high. No sooner had the little man got out of the casket than he began to grow at an alarming rate and in a matter of moments Reay was faced with the giant figure of none other than the Devil himself.

'Well,' boomed the Devil, 'what do you think of this?'

Reay was frightened, but he was also quick-witted. Assuming an air of nonchalance, he told the Devil that it was all very well to come out of the casket, but could he make himself small enough to get back in? The Devil was too vain to ignore Reay's taunting. He shrank himself smaller and smaller until once again, he was small enough to fit in through the hole in the casket. Reay picked up the tiny figure, rammed him into the casket and jammed a stone into the hole to plug it tightly. The Devil was trapped, and Reay had saved his own soul for another day.

the swans of Loch Sunart

Many years ago, it is said that the son of a chieftain who lived by Loch Sunart lost his heart to a beautiful girl. She was the daughter of a poor crofter. The young lad loved everything about her; her long shining hair, her slender, elegant neck, her ivory white skin and they way she bowed her head gracefully and smiled whenever he paid her a compliment. The two young lovers would meet every day on the shore of the loch and while away the hours together, holding hands and whispering loving words to each other as they wandered along the water's edge.

As far as the young lad was concerned, he had found his heart's desire and he wanted nothing more than to take her as his wife. But when he spoke to his mother about his sweetheart, she was enraged. She had dreams of her son finding a wife of noble birth, someone who would bring wealth and prestige to the family. She could not tolerate the thought of him marrying a crofter's daughter. She ordered him never to see or speak to the girl again.

But the young man ignored his mother's orders. He could not change his feelings for the girl and he could not stay away from her. He continued to meet with her every day, hoping that one day his mother would have a change of heart and let him marry her.

When his mother found out that she had been disobeyed, her fury turned to ruthlessness. She called upon a witch to cast a spell that would get rid of the crofter's daughter once and for all. The witch lay in wait by the lochside the next day and when the girl arrived, she turned her into a swan. The chieftain's son arrived soon after and waited on the shore until nightfall for his sweetheart to arrive, but she never appeared. Day after day, the young man returned to wait by the lochside, unwilling to give up hope that she might come back again, but after many weeks had passed, he realised that he had lost her. He had no idea where she might be, but she was gone and he could wait for her no longer.

Many weeks later, the chieftain's son was out by the loch with a hunting party. Catching sight of a swan resting at the water's edge, the young man aimed at it with his bow and shot it. The swan struggled to rise, but it was mortally wounded. It collapsed into the water at the edge of the loch. At the moment of death, the swan changed into the body of a beautiful young girl, and the chief's son realised what he had done. His heart was broken. As he watched the body of his sweetheart sink beneath the water, he made up his mind that they would never again be separated. He waded into the water beside her, drew his dagger and stabbed himself in the heart. As the two lovers disappeared from sight, all the other swans on the loch took flight. They would never return to Loch Sunart.

the saving of the forest

Most of the Great Caledonian Forest is now lost for ever, but hundreds of years ago it covered a vast area of Scotland, the dense cover of its mighty trees providing a sheltered habitat for a wide variety of wildlife, and hunting-grounds and timber for the people. Over time, the forest became diminished as trees were felled to create farmland and pasture, and their timber was used for fuel, building, and later, paper-making.

Forest fires have also taken their toll, particularly during the hotter, drier months of summer, and continue to pose a threat to the fragments of the Caledonian Forest that remain. At Badenoch in Speyside, there is still forest land in existence that was once part of the Caledonian Forest, but according to legend, its preservation was seriously threatened once upon a time.

Long ago, when the forest still stretched to the northern coasts, a monstrous witch came storming through the sky to destroy them by fire. According to one version of the legend, the witch was sent by the jealous King of Lochlan, but another tells us that she was a servant of Beira. Beira was the terrible goddess of winter, who raged with frustration every summer as Bride, who brought warmth and greenery to the land, reigned in her place.

In the hottest part of the summer, the witch came flying from a far island to vent her fury on the Caledonian Forest. Hiding from sight in a great, grey cloud that threw everything beneath it into murky shadow as it passed over, she crashed and banged out her rage for all to hear. As she reached the north of the land, she started to throw great balls of fire down, turning the parched undergrowth into a sheet of flame that set vast tracts of the forest ablaze. Day after day she returned to hurl destruction upon the land, and the terrible fires spread. The people of Badenoch grew more and more frightened as the furious hag moved closer to their lands, but they could not think how she could be stopped, for as long as she kept herself concealed in the thunder cloud, she was unassailable. Then a brave warrior stepped forwards. He had a plan to kill the witch, he said, but it would take him some time, and the people must be patient, whatever they saw or heard. The people agreed, for no-one else had volunteered their services, nor could anyone think of another plan, and so the warrior set about his task.

The warrior worked all day, and most of the night. He gathered up all the young animals from the fields, lambs, calves and foals, and took them to another place where their mothers could not see them. Before long the ewes, cows and mares began to complain piteously at being separated from their young, and the young animals, hungry and frightened and far from their mothers, let out their own cries of distress. As more and more young animals were separated, the noise of their distress grew louder. It continued without a break all through the night, and was terrible to hear. The people could not sleep for the noise of the grieving creatures, and would have reunited the mothers with their babies at once, had they not promised their patience to the warrior.

At last, having completed the first part of his plan, the warrior took up his spear. He positioned himself on the highest place in the district and waited. All around him, people gathered to watch. As the first glimmer of sunlight appeared in the east, a terrible thundering started up, far off in the distance, and the people knew at once that the witch was coming. The thunder grew louder and the sky began to darken on the horizon as she drew nearer. Soon the people could see smoke rising from new fires that she had started not many miles away. The hunter balanced his spear on his shoulder, gazed up at the sky, and waited. All around him, the bleating of sheep and lambs, the lowing of cattle and their calves and the whinnying of the mares and their foals rose to a cacophony. The sky grew darker and darker.

Inside her thunder cloud in the skies above Badenoch, the witch heard the animals' cries, stopped her fire-throwing, and wondered. What made them make such a noise? Was there something down there more terrible than she was? At last she could contain her curiosity no longer. She stuck her head out from the great grey-black billows of the cloud to take a look. On his hillock down below, the warrior was ready for her. At the first sight of her, he took aim with his spear. Then, with the sureness and strength of a champion, he threw his spear high into the air and it hit its mark. The spear sank deep into the witch's flesh, sending her shrieking and screaming into flight. The thunder cloud tore in two behind her and torrents of rain poured down from it, dowsing the flames and stopping the fires in their tracks. The Forest of Badenoch was saved.

monsters on Land and in water

the Loch ness monster

The most famous monster in Scotland is the beast that is said to live in the deep dark waters of Loch Ness. Affectionately known as Nessie, the monster is generally referred to as 'she', although there has never been an opportunity for anyone to determine the sex of this mythical creature. Nessie attracts visitors from all over the world, tourists, reporters and scientific investigators, and over the years has been subjected to more camera surveillance than any 'reality TV' programme participant is ever likely to have to endure. In spite of this, she remains elusive, guarding her privacy carefully in the hidden murky depths of the loch, rewarding the thousands of hopeful spectators who come to see her with no more than the occasional tantalising glimpse of what she might, or might not, look like.

The first written record of a beast in Loch Ness is in Saint Adamnan's biography of Saint Columba, which was written in the seventh century AD. According to Adamnan, Saint Columba was walking along the shore of the loch in 565 when he caught sight of an enormous creature in the water, ready to attack a man who was swimming there. Saint Columba ordered the beast to depart in the name of God, and it obeyed him. On another occasion Saint Columba encountered the creature again, lying in wait for a victim. Saint Columba commanded the monster never to harm a human being again, and since then, there have been no reports of the Loch Ness monster having threatened anyone.

Over the years, the Loch Ness monster seems to have surfaced from time to time, giving rise to a number of stories about the beast in the loch, but it was only in the twentieth century that Nessie's name came to real prominence. In the 1930s, a road was built alongside the northern shore of the loch. This brought a growth in the number of people visiting the area and also afforded passers-by a clear view of the loch from their cars. In 1933, Nessie hit the headlines of the *Inverness Courier*. A couple who lived in the district claimed to have seen an enormous creature thrashing about in the surface waters of the loch. The article in the *Courier* marked the beginning of Nessie's meteoric rise to fame. It was not long before she had allegedly been sighted on land, casually crossing the road by the loch one day in early summer. Loch Ness Monster fever rapidly spread and Nessie became national headlines as groups of people swarmed to the shores of Loch Ness hoping to see, or catch, the creature who dwelt therein. In August of that year, when the fever was at its peak, there were no less than nine alleged sightings of the monster in the water. In July 1934, there were at least eight more. Less than a year later, however, the first wave of monster-hunting began to peter out after some plaster-casts of large animal footprints, which were said to belong to the monster, were exposed as hoaxes. How many of the claimed sightings had been fakes?

In spite of the scepticism of many, interest in the possibility of a mysterious creature dwelling in the loch did not go away entirely. Sightings continued to be reported from time to time in the years that followed, and in the

1960s, monster fever seemed to take a hold of the public imagination once again. With the resurgence in public interest came another increase in the number of alleged sightings. The summer of 1966 was particularly busy. The 1970s and '80s seem to have been a time of general cynicism, or short-sightedness, for scarcely a handful of sightings were recorded, but in the 1990s, armed with the wonders of sophisticated photography, video cameras, etc., members of the public took up the hunt once more.

So, if the Loch Ness monster does exist, or has ever existed, what sort of creature might she be? In the days of Saint Columba, she was seen (or imagined) to be one of the kelpies, or water horses, mythical creatures which were believed to prey on unsuspecting human victims, particularly children, luring them onto their backs before dragging them down into the water, never to be seen again. In more recent times, she has been described as having between one and three humps, which are somewhere between four and forty feet in length and are commonly said to resemble an upturned boat. She has been said to have a long tail and a long neck, around six feet long. Her mouth may be approximately one foot wide. When submerging and moving off, she makes a great splash and leaves a v-shaped wake behind her. Of course although the creature is commonly referred to as *the* Loch Ness monster (singular), it cannot be possible that there has only been one creature surviving nearly fifteen hundred years since the days of Saint Columba. There must have been, at least, a succession of breeding pairs over the centuries, and the fact that on a few occasions not one, but two 'monster wakes' have allegedly been spotted simultaneously, seems to support this theory. The one identifiable creature which Nessie can be said to resemble most closely is the plesiosaur, which was a carnivorous marine reptile of the Jurassic and Cretaceous periods. Plesiosaurs could grow to around forty feet in length, had long necks and turtle-shaped bodies, and had paddle-like flippers to propel themselves through the water. There are many people who believe that Nessie is a plesiosaur, and although the survival of a family of such creatures in one isolated place in Scotland is hard to explain when all the others became extinct sixty-five million years ago, there have been attempts to demonstrate that such a thing is possible. One theory suggests that some plesiosaur eggs, long frozen in some deep, cold recess of the loch, could have thawed out and hatched to start the new dynasty. The cynics continue to contest the theory by stating that the loch does not have an adequate supply of food for such a creature, and so argument is met with counter-argument *ad nauseam*.

Loch Ness is huge, dark, and deep. Much of its waters are literally unfathomable, and this is perhaps the biggest hurdle, both for all those who wish to prove Nessie's existence, and those who wish to disprove it. The mystery is kept at the forefront of the public's imagination with boat trips and sightseeing tours around the loch on offer for visiting tourists, and a Loch Ness Monster Exhibition at the local visitor centre. Alleged sightings are faithfully recorded in detail, and video footage of gloomy, unidentifiable shapes in the water is studied closely by enthusiasts and sceptics alike. For the real Nessie fan, the opportunity to look for the monster on webcam from the comfort of their own home has taken the hunt into the twenty-first century. The legend continues to grow.

morag of Loch morar

Loch Morar is not as large in surface area as Loch Ness, but the water there is deeper, and it is said that hundreds of feet below the surface of the loch lives another monster, who has come to be known as Morag. Morag has not reached the same dizzy heights of stardom as Nessie, and her history is not as long, but for those who are fascinated with mythical creatures of the deep, the possibility of her existence is no less exciting.

The earliest recorded sightings of the Loch Morar monster date from the second half of the nineteenth century. From time to time, fishermen out on the loch, or walkers making their way along its rocky shores, would claim to have seen one or more dark humps in the water, like upturned boats. Superstitions about death and dying were still very much a part of life in the Highlands in those days, and some said that these strange sights were omens of death, ghostly boats that warned of some tragedy to come. Others were not so sure, for they were convinced that the humps were a part of something living, some mysterious creature that rarely allowed itself to be seen. Years passed, and the rumours of the creature grew slowly. Eventually, as Nessie had done, this creature acquired a name, but still she remained reclusive, and she is still less sought-after than Nessie.

Many of the people who claimed to have seen Morag were fishing on the loch at the time. The sight of her hump (or humps), appearing and disappearing in the water, have caused great perplexity to a number of people over the years. In the 1960s, Morag was allegedly responsible for ruining an entire day's fishing for two young men. They were rowing out into the loch, and saw what the thought was a smooth, rounded rocky outcrop sticking out of the water, so they started to navigate their way round the obstacle with care. Their boat was hired, and they had no wish to pay for any damages they might incur with a careless bump. They were only half way round this miniature island when it suddenly moved, then sank, bumping into their little boat on the way down and making ripples of such a size that they almost capsized. Forgetting all about fishing, or the price they had paid for a day's boat hire, the two young men rowed back to shore as quickly as possible. There, with wide eyes and white faces, they returned the boat to its puzzled owner, muttering as they did so about the dangers 'out there'.

Descriptions of Morag, who has been seen mostly in the water, but also, on at least one occasion, on shore, make her sound very similar in appearance to her famous friend in Loch Ness. She is dark in colour – brownish-black or black. Her skin is bumpy, like that of a reptile. She has been variously described as having one, two, three or four humps, and it is thought that she is around thirty feet long. Like Nessie, she has a long neck. One man who claimed to have seen her also said that he found her footprints in some soft ground on the shore, and they were diamond-shaped. A monster spotter with artistic leanings, Dr George Cooper, painted her portrait in 1958, but as Morag rarely reveals more of herself than a hump here and a neck there, it is hard to tell whether Dr Cooper managed to capture a true likeness. Those who have the time, energy and enthusiasm to continue the search will maybe be rewarded with the chance to see for themselves one day in the future.

Loch Morar is more remote and less easily accessible than Loch Ness, and most of the time, Morag is left in peace. Every now and then, another alleged sighting is logged in the records of keen cryptozoologists, but most visitors to the area barely give her more than a passing thought, and her presence is not advertised. For those who live close to Loch Morar, it is probably a good thing that Morag has not drawn the same attention to herself as Nessie. There is no monster exhibition, and local people are, for the most part, reluctant to exploit the monster rumours in any way.

But monster enthusiasts are a die-hard bunch, and for them the legend lives on, even if it breathes more quietly than the legend of Nessie. And the theories about what she might be are much the same; like Nessie, she is now most commonly believed to be a plesiosaur – it may be possible, some say, that Nessie and Morag are related. It has even been suggested that far, far underground, there is a long water-filled tunnel that connects Loch Ness with Loch Morar and that the Loch Ness Monster and the Loch Morar Monster are one and the same creature, travelling between the two sites. Perhaps she likes to keep the visitors entertained. Or perhaps, in the way that all film stars do, the monster sometimes tires of all the cameras and attention. At times like these, we might imagine that she takes a break from life in Loch Ness and goes to Loch Morar to annoy a few fishermen for a change.

Nessie and Morag are the two most famous loch-dwelling monsters in Scotland, but, if we are to believe in their existence, we must also give some credence to the claims that in several other Scottish lochs – Loch Garten and Loch Oich, for example, similar creatures have been sighted. If all the claims are true, there could be as many as twenty loch monsters, perhaps even more!

the Linton worm

There are a number of references to 'worms' in traditional Scottish stories. The monster that is said to live in Loch Morar, for example, was once known as 'The Great Worm' and some versions of the story of Michael Scott and the serpent (below) refer to the beast as a worm. Several sites around the country are said to have been, once upon a time, the dwelling place of a worm. These worms were great serpents, which were said to terrorise the surrounding countryside, killing the farmers' animals and attacking humans. Some were believed to have magical powers. Others had rank, poisonous breath.

The story of the worm of Linton belongs to the Scottish Borders, where long ago, in Roxburghshire, it is said that a fearsome serpent used to live in a hollow on the slopes of Linton Hill near Jedburgh. For years the Linton worm blighted the lives of the people living in the district. Its breath was said to be so poisonous that if a man inhaled the slightest whiff of it, he faced instant death, so no-one dared approach it. Farmers stood by helplessly as their sheep and cattle dwindled in numbers, snapped up, one by one, by the ravenous jaws of the worm. No man had the courage to try to kill it, for it seemed like an impossible task, sure to end in death for anyone who attempted it.

Then a man called John Sommerville of Lauriston heard about the beast, and decided to come and see the worm for himself. Following the directions given to him be some people who lived nearby, Sommerville rode his horse cautiously towards the hollow where the terrible creature lay resting. He stopped his horse at a safe distance from the worm's lair and waited. The wind carried the scent of a human towards the sleeping beast, and slowly it woke up, and reared up its ugly head to find where the scent was coming from. Sommerville kept a tight hold of the horse's reins and remained perfectly still. At the sight of the man and the horse together, the worm seemed perplexed. It stretched out its neck and opened its jaws to their fullest extent, but it did not attack. It gave out a great puff of its fiery venomous breath, but Sommerville was too far away to feel its effects, and the poisonous gas dispersed in the air before it reached him. Still the serpent remained motionless, its jaws gaping helplessly. The sight gave Sommerville much food for thought. It was clear that although a single cow, or sheep, or even a man would make an easy mouthful for the beast, the prospect of man and horse together had it puzzled, for the two were more than its jaws could cope with.

As he turned and rode back home, a cunning plan was forming in Sommerville's mind. The next day, he went to the local blacksmith and asked him to make a special lance. The lance had to be much longer than such a weapon would normally be, for Sommerville had to keep a safe distance from the monster's breath. At the end of the lance was to be a spiked wheel made of the strongest iron.

When the lance had been finished to his satisfaction, Sommerville prepared to do battle. Taking his most loyal servant along with him, he rode into Jedburgh carrying his customised weapon and declared that soon the

Linton worm would be dead. Not surprisingly, his claims were met with jeers and derision, for what he claimed, according to the people of Jedburgh, was impossible. Nonetheless, a number of townsfolk followed him out to Linton Hill, and selecting a viewpoint as close to the worm's hollow as they dared go, settled down to watch the action.

Sommerville rode closer to the worm's lair. His servant followed on foot. Sommerville reined in his horse and the servant took a ball of peat dipped in pitch from the bag he carried on his back, and stuck it firmly onto the spiked wheel at the end of Sommerville's lance. They moved a little closer. Just as before, the serpent caught the scent of human flesh and reared up its head. Just as it had done before, it stretched out its neck and opened its jaws to their fullest extent. At a signal from his master, the servant set fire to the peat ball on Sommerville's lance, and set it spinning. Sommerville spurred his horse into a gallop, charged up to the open-mouthed worm, and thrust his lance as far as he could down its throat. The serpent writhed in fury and pain as the fiery peat ball seared his gullet and the spikes pierced his flesh, but it had been mortally wounded, and after one or two moments of desperate struggling, it stopped moving and died.

Sir John Sommerville had become a hero, and as reward for his courage, he was knighted, becoming the first Baron of Linton. At Linton Kirk nearby, a stone was carved to commemorate the great occasion when the people of Linton were saved from the worm. And on the landscape of Linton Hill, the strange undulating marks caused by the worm as it writhed and struggled before death still remain.

michael scott and the serpent

Michael Scott was a man of great learning who lived in Scotland in the thirteenth century. He was believed by many to be a great wizard, who performed a great number of astonishing feats with his magical powers, and there are several legends told about his life and the wonders that he performed. Michael Scott had a number of magical helpers whom he could order to carry out great tasks for him. According to some people, these helpers were imps, sent by the Devil to torment him with their endless requests for work to keep them busy. Other people believed the helpers to be fairy folk in his employ. Whenever the helpers finished a task that Michael Scott had set them, they would return for more work to do, and so great buildings were erected, rivers were bridged, causeways were built across stormy stretches of water, and so on.

The tale of how Michael tired of these helpers continually pestering him for work is familiar to many people, and of how he finally set an impossible and unending task to keep them occupied – that of constructing ropes of sand to build a rope ladder to the moon. Every time the task got underway, the tide came in and washed away all their work and so they were condemned to carry on with their fruitless labours for all eternity. But how did Michael Scott come about his magical powers?

Scott was born in the Scottish borders, but he travelled far and wide during the course of his life. His love of travel began when he was quite young, exploring the highways and byways of Scotland. The legend tells us that on one occasion, he set off from his home with two of his friends to travel northwards. Shunning the high road, they tramped across the wild countryside. They were climbing a hill, wondering if the view from the top might help them decide which way to go next, when they suddenly caught sight of a great white serpent. It writhed and zig-zagged up the hillside to where the three men stood, and soon they could hear the angry hiss from its forked tongue, and see its wide jaws opening, ready for attack. Scott's companions turned and fled, but Scott stood his ground and when the serpent was within feet of him, it reared up its head, preparing to devour him. Scott raised his walking staff and struck the serpent once, and then again, using all the strength he could summon. The force of the blows was so great that the serpent's body was severed in two places. When Scott stood back, he saw the serpent lying dead in three pieces on the ground before him. Cautiously, his companions crept back to see what had happened and were stunned to see the evidence of Scott's courage and strength. But neither of them was willing to linger a moment longer, and so, having congratulated Scott and thanked him heartily for saving their lives, they urged him to hurry on. It was getting late and they needed to find somewhere to spend the night.

The three men found congenial lodgings with an old woman who lived in a cottage a few miles further on. As they all sat down to supper, Scott's companions told their hostess about the great adventure of the day. To their surprise, she did not congratulate them as heartily as they had expected.

'Did you leave the serpent lying where it was killed?' she wanted to know.

'Why, yes,' said Scott. 'We saw no need to move it and we had no wish to touch it again.'

'You must go back to where you found it, and you must hurry!' the woman said. 'It is no ordinary beast. Folk around here thought it had been killed once before. It attacked a man who used to live in these parts, but he was too quick for it and cut it in two with his sword. It lay there without moving for some hours, but then all of a sudden its two parts began to move together. When the two parts were joined up but still bleeding, the beast slid into the stream, and the water must have healed it, for the bleeding stopped and it became whole again without a scar to show for it! Believe me, it was not long before that creature was strong enough to take out a terrible revenge on the poor man who had left it for dead!'

'But we are moving on in the morning,' protested Scott, ' and we will have no need to return to this place again. Why should I be afraid of the serpent's revenge?'

'Because it will find you, wherever you are,' said the old woman. 'There is only one way to save yourself. You must go back, as quickly as you can, and remove the middle part of the serpent's body. Without it, the beast will not be able to make itself whole again.'

Scott hesitated, for he had no wish to go back out into the darkness. He was already tired from the day's exertions, and he was terrified in case he might be too late. But he knew that he must go while he had the chance, and so he left his companions warming themselves by the old woman's fire and set out on the lonely trek with all speed. Luck was with him, for he found the spot without any difficulty and to his great relief, he saw that the three pieces of the serpent's body had not yet moved. He snatched the middle segment up into his arms and stumbled away, all the time peering anxiously ahead for the comforting sight of the lights of the cottage in the distance.

The old woman was waiting at the door to greet him.

'You have got it!' she cried, with obvious delight. She took the middle part of the serpent's body from him and carried it over to the fire, where she placed it in a big pot standing over the flames. Her eyes glistened with excitement as she stood over the pot, listening as the serpent's flesh began to sizzle.

'Why are you cooking it?' asked Scott.

'It is the only thing to do to destroy it,' declared the woman. 'Besides, it will make a nourishing dish for my supper tomorrow.'

The night drew on and Scott's two companions declared that they would go to bed. The old woman showed them into another room, then returned to the kitchen, where Scott was resting his aching limbs in a chair beside the fire.

'Are you not ready for sleep yet?' she asked him.

'Not yet,' said Scott. 'My legs are painful, and I feel quite unwell. The heat from the fire is comforting. May I stay here? I might be able to fall asleep in this chair, but a cold bed will do me no good.'

'Very well,' said the woman. 'If you are here, then I can go to bed and leave you to mind the pot.' She nodded towards the fire, where the serpent's flesh was still cooking. Once again, Scott was aware that the woman, although outwardly calm, could hardly contain her excitement. He was sure that there was something she was not telling him about the unusual dish that she was cooking.

'What should I do when the meat is cooked?' he asked.

'Just make sure that it does not burn,' said the old woman. 'Otherwise leave it well alone. I shall come back when it is cooked and do what needs to be done, so you need not touch it.'

The old woman went to bed. Scott dozed fitfully in the chair, while the pot containing the serpent meat bubbled gently on the fire beside him. Some time later, he could smell that the meat was cooked. Not a sound came from the old woman's bedroom, and although Scott knew that she would have wished him to wake her, he rose from his chair quietly and lifted the lid off the pot. The middle part of the serpent's body had stewed in its own juices and was now tender and ready to eat. Scott dipped his finger into the steaming liquid surrounding the meat, and tasted it. The liquid was scalding hot and Scott jumped back in pain, dropping the lid of the pot that he was holding in his other hand with a clatter. The sound woke the old woman, and she came hurrying from her bed. Scott was still sucking his finger when she came into the kitchen.

' Did you taste the juice from the pot?' she cried, her face full of dismay.

'I did,' said Scott. 'And why not? It was I who killed the serpent, after all. And now I know why you were so anxious that I should leave it alone, for I know things now that I have never known before, about the past, the present and the future. And simply by wishing it to happen, I have made the pain in my aching legs and scalded finger vanish.'

'You have more power in you than you could ever have imagined,' said the old woman. 'I must confess that was it was the power I hoped to gain by being the first to take a taste from the pot. But I will admit that you deserve it more than I do. Use it carefully, and think kindly of me when you move on, for if I had not warned you about the serpent, you would have been facing death.'

Scott promised the old woman that he would remember her with gratitude, and she returned to her room to sleep again. She had been deprived of the magical powers she had so often dreamed of, but at least she had a good meal to look forward to the next day.

Early in the morning, Scott and his companions bade farewell to the old woman and resumed their journey.

'We have a long walk ahead of us today,' complained on of the men. 'My legs are still tired from yesterday and the weather is bitterly cold. How I wish we were at our destination already!'

Scott straddled his walking staff and beckoned the others to hold on to his coat tails. With a few whispered words, the staff shot up into the sky, taking the three men with it.

'There is no need for walking today,' Scott cried to his startled companions as they soared through the clouds. 'We will be at our journey's end well before nightfall!'

The exploits of Michael Scott would often leave people gasping in wonderment. Many people were impressed by his powers, some were very envious of him, but many more were deeply suspicious and afraid. Was he dabbling in black sorcery? Might he be in league with the Devil? It is said that Scott never divulged the source of his powers to anyone until he was old and frail, and close to death. As he lay dying, he was questioned one more time about his powers, for the people around him were anxious to know whether the Devil had claimed his soul. Scott did not answer them directly.

'When I am dead,' he said, 'cut my heart from my body and place it on a pole outside. If a raven comes down from the sky and carries my heart away, you will know that I am bound for hell. If a dove takes it away, you will know that I am going to heaven.'

Not long after that, Michael Scott took his last breath. When his body was cold, they cut his heart out, placed it on a pole outside the house, and waited and watched. Some moments later a raven appeared in the distance. The watchers gasped in horror as it flew towards Scott's heart, but at the last minute, it changed course and flew off into the trees. When the raven had gone, a dove appeared in its place. It flew down without any hesitation, plucked the heart from the pole and carried it off in its beak.

the big grey man of ben macdhui

Ben Macdhui is the highest peak in the Cairngorms, and the second highest in Scotland. From its summit, the climber is afforded a magnificent panorama of the surrounding peaks; Cairngorm, Ben Avon and Cairn Toul. To the north west, the River Spey passes through Aviemore on its way to the Moray Firth. To the east, the Dee flows towards Ballater, Aboyne and Aberdeen. The mountain is popular with climbers who visit the region from many different countries, and its slopes offer a number of routes that are both challenging and rewarding, even to experienced mountaineers. But Ben Macdhui is well-known not only for its beauty and the sport that it offers its visitors. For over a century now, there has been much speculation that there may be something frightening lurking on Ben Macdhui. Over this period, several climbers claim to have witnessed a mysterious presence on the mountain; many believe it to be a physical one. This presence has been named Am Fear Liath Mor, more commonly known as The Big Grey Man.

On remote mountain slopes, far from the noise and bustle of centres of population, it is easy to give full reign to the imagination and let the mind wander to strange apparitions and monsters. There are plenty of things that the mountain climber encounters to provide fuel for the mind's journey; strange echoes in gullies, tricks of the light, shapes in the mist, ominous shadows cast as the sun moves across the unfamiliar landscape. Human beings are social animals, and solitude is alien to most of us. It can alter one's perceptions, especially in an unfamiliar environment, and fear of real, physical and recognisable danger can find itself accompanied by a fear of unidentifiable, intangible threats, which come from a realm far removed from man's knowledge of the physical world and its nature.

It is easier to dismiss the legends of monstrous apparitions in the mountains around the world than it is to give credence to them. The existence of the creatures in these legends has never been proved beyond doubt by material evidence or scientific fact. The Yeti in the Himlayas, Bigfoot in North America, and the Spectre of the Brocken in Germany are all similar in this respect; they are beasts seen, but not captured, perceived but not touched. Some believe that there is a physical presence of some kind where these creatures have allegedly been seen. Most people, on the other hand, do not, and react to the legends with scepticism or derision. The Yeti and Bigfoot feature in cartoons from time to time, as cuddly figures of fun. The Spectre of the Brocken in dismissed in more scientific fashion, as a shadowy illusion created by sunlight and mist.

The Big Grey Man of Ben Macdhui, like the other monstrous apparitions, has allegedly been seen and heard on a number of different occasions. But there is another more sinister aspect to the Grey Man, which the other apparitions do not share. The Big Grey Man's presence is not perceived by the physical senses alone. It can make itself felt in the spirits, in a manner that is generally claimed to be very disturbing. It is alleged that the Grey Man exerts a strong psychic influence upon those who encounter him. And several climbers, after having undergone the experience, have been reluctant to return to the mountain.

The first time the possible existence of the Big Grey Man of Ben Macdhui was mentioned in Scotland was in 1925. Norman Collie, a professor in Chemistry from London and an experienced and well-respected mountaineer, related his story to members of the Cairngorm Club at their Annual General Meeting. He recalled a solo climb on the mountain in 1891, and said that as he was making his way back down the mountainside from the summit through the mist, he became aware of the sound of footsteps behind him. For every three or four steps that the professor took, he heard one of these footsteps, as if whoever – or whatever – was following him taking much larger strides than himself. At first, he dismissed the sounds as nonsense, for he could see nothing, but as he continued downwards he could still hear them. At this point he was overwhelmed by a feeling of terror, and in blind panic, took flight, descending the rest of the mountain with more concern for speed than safety on the treacherous terrain.

The experience had left him badly shaken, and determined that he would never climb Ben Macdhui alone again, for there was something 'very queer' about the higher slopes of the mountain.

Collie had told this story once before, some years earlier in New Zealand, and it had been greeted with a moderate degree of interest and some understandable scepticism. But when Dr A M Kellas had heard about it, he was more than moderately interested in Collie's experience. Dr Kellas was another well-known figure in mountaineering circles, much respected for his achievements climbing in the Himalayas, who later died during the first expedition to Mount Everest in 1921–22. When Kellas heard Collie's story, he wrote to him to tell him of his own experience. Kellas had been on Ben Macdhui with his brother, and had been hammering out crystals from some rocks quite close to the summit when they had become aware of a large figure descending from above, out of the mist. The two men had then, like Collie, succumbed to a terrible feeling of fear and had been compelled to flee.

We do not know why Collie waited 34 years to tell his story to the Cairngorm Club, but it is reasonable to assume that he might have felt apprehensive about the reception it might get. Perhaps the letter from Kellas helped to give Collie the courage to relate his account of the experience. But at any rate, when he did finally speak out in 1925, he would know that there was at least one other knowledgeable, reasonable and experienced man who had testified to having had a similar encounter. Both men had spent extended amounts of time in remote mountain regions and consequently knew all too well the tricks that could be played on the mind when a person was alone, cold and tired. They were also familiar with the strange sights and sounds of such places; shadows in the mist, falling rocks, echoes and suchlike. But both strenuously denied that the phenomenon they had witnessed was anything like this.

There have been several reports of alleged encounters with the Big Grey Man since then. Some of them, undoubtedly, have been fantasy, or hoax. Others cannot be dismissed so easily. Some people claim to have heard strange voices, speaking in a foreign tongue, which has been said to resemble either Gaelic, or Urdu. Others have said that they could hear hauntingly beautiful music. Alleged sightings vary from a vague description of a hazy, large, upright figure to a more precise picture of something akin to the Sasquatch or Yeti.

In 1944, Captain Sir Hugh Rankin claimed to have met and spoken with the Big Grey Man on two separate occasions. According to Sir Hugh, who was a Buddhist himself, the Grey Man was a Bodhisattwa. (A Bodhisattwa is a being in an advanced degree of incarnation, next to that of a Buddha, who has achieved enlightenment and acts as a guide to others in their progress towards the same.) Sir Hugh was humbled, but unafraid. His experience of the Big Grey Man was apparently wholly benign.

But most other climbers who have tales to tell of the Big Grey Man or of out-of-the-ordinary experiences on Ben Macdhui have shared feelings that are much different from those felt by Sir Hugh Rankin. Fear, sudden and overwhelming, has been commonly reported and openly admitted, even by hardened men of the outdoors. Sudden, terrible feelings of depression have also been described on a number of occasions. In some men's experience, these feelings have rapidly led to thoughts of suicide and frightening compulsions to self harm by falling or jumping off a ledge or into a gully. This power that the phenomenon of the Grey Man seems to exert over people's minds is what makes it uniquely sinister and dangerous. Perhaps, knowing something about the phenomenon, the fear of an encounter with the Big Grey Man that has both triggered and inflamed the imaginations of many climbers on the slopes of Ben Macdhui, affecting their mood and convincing them that such an encounter has taken place. But that does not explain why Collie and Kellas felt as they did, on separate occasions and quite independently of each other. Nor will all climbers since then have known about the phenomenon before they set off up the mountain.

The phenomenon may be nothing more than a collection of misperceptions, or optical and aural illusions. It may be hallucination induced by fatigue, or hysteria. Norman Collie may have had a panic attack. Dr Kellas may have seen his own shadow in the mist. But their refusal to dismiss their experience as illusion or panic persisted until their deaths. Furthermore, there are several people still alive who claim to have experienced the Big Grey Man – whatever it is. And like Collie and Kellas, those among them whose claims were made in good faith are unlikely ever to be convinced that there is not 'something up there.'

visitors to the fairy realm

Belief in fairies was prevalent in Scotland in days gone by. Although they were spiritual beings, fairies were thought to resemble human beings in many ways; their physical appearance was similar, they lived together in social communities, they ate, drank, danced and sang, they could be kind, or malicious, charitable or unforgiving. Fairies were invisible to the human eye for most of the time, but when they did allow themselves to be seen, they were most commonly described as slender and pale, with gold-red hair, dressed in green. Most of them were, or appeared as women.

Opinions differed as to what, or who, the fairies were. Some people believed they were fallen angels, or demons. Others thought that they were the spirits of the dead. Other people simply saw them as another class of being, inhabitants of a world that existed separately from the human world, but from which they, at least, could come and go as they pleased.

Few people thought of fairies as either intrinsically good or bad. They were generally believed to be capable of behaviour ranging from one extreme to the other. But it was always considered better to be cautious rather than casual about fairies. They could steal food, if it was left unprotected, and what was worse, they could steal an unbaptised child, and leave a fretful, wizened changeling in its place. It was generally considered prudent to take precautions against such things happening, with the use of charms against the fairy magic, or bribes of milk and food to appease them.

The fairy realm was most commonly thought to be a subterranean world, which the fairies reached through hidden entrances in hills, mountains, rocks and sometimes caves. It was generally thought to be a place filled with light, and with music, for the fairies were skilled musicians. It was a place where time seemed to stand still, or to pass very slowly. It was inaccessible to most human beings, and traditionally, those who did find their way into the fairy realm were unlikely to come out again. If they did, their lives were changed.

thomas the rhymer

Thomas the Rhymer is a very 'weel-kent' figure in Scots story-telling and poetry, a man who is believed to have prophesied many major events in Scottish history while he was alive. He was said to speak the truth always, hence the other name by which he is commonly known, True Thomas. Although Thomas the Rhymer is a legendary figure, and is said to have lived in various parts of the country, it is most commonly believed that the legends originally grew up around a poet who lived in the Scottish borders during the thirteenth century. Thomas was born Thomas Learmont of Ercildoune. Ercildoune was a village now known as Earlston, situated in the Scottish border country, not far from the towns of Galashiels and Melrose. According to the most famous legend of his life, Thomas was not born with the gift of prophecy, but acquired it from the queen of the fairies.

Thomas was out walking in the Eildon Hills near his home one day, and he stopped to rest by Huntly Water, under the shade of the Eildon Tree. As he lay half-dozing in the shade, something caught his eye, and he turned to see a beautiful woman, clad in green silk and velvet, riding towards him on a white horse which had a bridle festooned with bright silver bells. There was something extraordinary about this woman, and Thomas was captivated by her beauty. As soon as he caught sight of her, he jumped to his feet, removed his hat and bowed before her. He thought she must be the Queen of Heaven, and addressed her as such. But the woman told him that she was not the Queen of Heaven, but the Queen of Elfland, where the fairies lived. Thomas was surprised to find that she knew his name, but he was even more perplexed when she declared that she had come expressly to seek him out. She dared him to kiss her on the lips, and Thomas did not hesitate. The Queen of Elfland now had him in her power.

'Now,' said the queen, 'you must come with me to Elfinland, where you will serve me for seven years, for good or for bad.'

Thomas was entranced with his new acquaintance and climbed up behind her on the horse without another word. They rode on and on, until they were far from any place familiar to Thomas, and it seemed as if the journey might never end. When the horse finally drew to a halt, the lush, green summer countryside was nowhere to be seen and they were in a barren desert. The Queen dismounted with Thomas.

'Now,' she said, 'I have three wonders to show you.' She pointed to three different roads that lay ahead of them, each going in a different direction. The first road was overgrown with thorns and briars. Travel along such a road would be painful and difficult, for the thorns made it almost impossible to make one's way along it.

'That road,' the Queen told Thomas, 'is the road to Righteousness. There are few men who choose to take it.'

The second road was wide and easy to travel on. Lilies, their heads heavy with scented pollen, grew all along the verges.

'That road,' the Queen said, 'is the road to Hell, although many people do not believe it and mistake it for the road to Heaven.'

The third road stretched ahead through a green landscape, covered in a dense blanket of ferns.

'That road,' said the Queen, 'is the road to Elfinland, where we are going. While you are in Elfinland, Thomas, you must remember one thing. You must never speak. If you utter a single word, you will never be able to return to your own land.'

The Queen and Thomas travelled on into the night. It was a difficult journey, for they had to cross rivers and rocky countryside in the darkness, and there was no moon to light their way. Then they came to a river that was unlike all the others. As they waded through the murky waters, Thomas could just make out that the water was blood red.

'This is the river that carries away all the blood that is shed on the earth,' the Queen told him.

They rode on until at last they game to a garden, which was full of trees laden with fruit of all kinds. The Queen went up to an apple tree and plucked a plump, red fruit from its branches and handed it to Thomas.

'Take this in payment,' she said to him. 'Eat it, and you will have a tongue that can never lie.'

Thomas took the apple from the Queen and ate it, overawed at having been given such a priceless gift.

'Now Thomas,' said the Queen, 'remember, not another word.' Thomas nodded. They mounted the horse and rode on, deep into the fairy realm.

Thomas was given a suit of green clothes and green velvet shoes, and so began his service to the Fairy Queen. The time he spent in Elfinland passed quickly, and it seemed to Thomas that only a few days had gone by when the Queen summoned him to her and told him that he was free to go. But time in Elfinland is not the same as time in the land of the humans, and the Queen told him that when he returned to his own land, he would find that he had been away for seven years. As he took his leave of the Fairy Queen, she bade him a fond farewell, but said that she would see him again.

'I will come again and call you back to Elfinland,' she told him. 'When the day comes, you will know.'

And so Thomas the Rhymer returned to the land of humans, and not a word did he say to anyone of what he has seen and learned during his stay in Elfinland. His reputation as a prophet soon became known far and wide, and the accuracy with which he was able to foretell what would happen in the future was astonishing. He lived a contented life. He was a respected member of the community in which he lived, and his honesty and forthrightness were much appreciated by all those who knew him. He did not know when the day would come for him to return to the Fairy Queen, but he bided his time patiently, knowing that some day, a sign would be given to him.

And so it happened that one day, a young lad came running into the village, saying that he had seen a white hart and a white hind coming out of the forest nearby. Several of the villagers gathered together and went to see if what the boy was saying was true and sure enough, at the edge of the wood, they saw two white deer standing calmly beneath the trees, watching and waiting. The villagers called upon Thomas and told him what they had seen. They wanted to know if the unusual sight was an omen. When Thomas had listened to their news, he smiled, for he knew what it meant, but he did not explain. He simply bade his friends an affectionate farewell and walked off to the edge of the forest where the two creatures stood. Then all three moved off together and disappeared into the trees. Thomas the Rhymer was never seen again.

What happened to the Reverend Robert Kirk?

Robert Kirk was born in Aberfoyle in Perthshire, and was the son of the Episcopalian minister there. He succeeded in his father's footsteps and became a minister himself, first at Balquidder and then at Aberfoyle. He was a devout and scholarly man, but he was also the seventh son of a seventh son and as such, is said to have possessed psychic gifts. The existence of another plane peopled by beings imperceptible to the ordinary man intrigued Kirk, and his studies into this hidden universe were eventually published in 1692, entitled The Secret Commonwealth of Elves, Fauns and Faeries. Belief in the existence of numerous categories of supernatural beings was deeply rooted in Gaelic culture, and Kirk, in spite of his position as a God-fearing man, saw no need to deny his own beliefs. *The Secret Commonwealth* combined intellectual, pseudo-scientific analysis with a curiously frank assumption on the part of the author that a supernatural realm, inhabited by beings which interacted with and acted upon man, was a fact to be accepted without question.

The Secret Commonwealth is what Kirk is best remembered for, and he died not long after it was published. His life up until that point had been unremarkable. His first wife had died at a young age, but although it was a sad event it was not unusual. In those days, death was a more frequent visitor to people's homes than it is now. Kirk remarried after he took up the ministry at Aberfoyle, and his wife became pregnant with their first child in 1692. Then tragedy struck. Kirk was out walking in the countryside round Aberfoyle and had reached a hillock known as the Dun Sidhe, or the Fairy Knoll, when he collapsed and died.

The grieving family had their beloved's body returned to them, and they laid it to rest. And there the matter might have ended. But Kirk's interest in psychic phenomena was well known, and the fact that he had died so unexpectedly at the Fairy Knoll seemed like a strange coincidence. A legend about the good reverend was born, which outlived and outshone the ordinary story of his life. It was said that Robert Kirk was not dead. He had not been taken by sudden heart failure, or brain trauma, or any other fatal bodily calamity. He had been taken alive by the fairies, spirited away into the depths of the Fairy Knoll, and in place of his body, the kidnappers had left a fairy stock, in likeness of him.

According to the legend, Kirk had only one chance

to escape from the fairy realm, and that was at the forthcoming christening of his baby. Shortly after his burial, Kirk appeared before his cousin, Grahame of Duchray, and told him what had happened. He explained that he had fallen into a faint while out walking, and that while he was unconscious, the fairies had taken him.

Kirk begged Duchray to help him to escape, and instructed him on what had to be done. At the child's christening, Duchray would see Kirk appear a second time in front of him. In order to banish the fairy spell which had been cast over him, Duchray had to take an iron dagger (iron was a powerful talisman against fairy magic) and throw it over Kirk's head. Duchray agreed to do what was asked of him, and Kirk disappeared.

The day of the christening arrived, and Duchray waited for his moment, dagger at the ready. But when he caught sight of the ghostly figure of Robert Kirk, his courage failed him, and he could not bring himself to carry out the task he had been set. Kirk turned his back on his cousin and disappeared, back to the Fairy Realm in the depths of the hill, and was never seen again.

the fiddlers of tomnahurich

There was once a pair of musicians, who lived in Inverness-shire. They were down on their luck, and in spite of their considerable skills in playing the fiddle, had not found an audience to pay them well for a long time. And so it was that when they met an old man who said he could find them a night's work, they gladly took him up on his offer. The old man took the fiddlers up the hill at Tomnahurich, and in through an entrance in the hillside that they had never seen before. They followed him in and the entrance closed behind them. The fiddlers found themselves in a bright place, richly decorated and full of the sound of laughter, where beautiful slender women, handsome men and delicate-featured children were feasting. There was food and drink in abundance, and the two musicians were invited to take their fill before the dancing began. When they had eaten all that they wanted, they tuned up their fiddles and started to play. The dancing went on all night, and the fiddlers had as good a time as the revellers did. When it seemed at last that everyone had had enough, the old man paid them well for their trouble with a bag of gold coins, and ushered them out of the mysterious place into the grey light of dawn.

The fiddlers made their way back down the hillside in fine spirits, but when they got into town they were greatly taken aback by what they saw. New buildings had sprung up here and there, and the place looked completely different. They walked through the town without seeing a soul that they recognised, and that was most unusual. Everyone was dressed very strangely, and several people whom they passed commented on the fiddler's 'old-fashioned' clothing. They heard the church bell ringing, calling people to worship, and decided to seek comfort in the familiar rituals of the church service. They walked into the church and settled themselves in their pew, still puzzled to notice that there was not a familiar face in the congregation. The minister came up to the pulpit and the fiddlers stood up with the other members of the congregation, ready to begin the morning's worship. But when the minister began to speak, and mentioned the name of God, the two fiddlers crumbled to dust.

They had not been away for just one night. They had been kept in the Fairy Realm for one hundred years. And the old man who had invited them inside was none other than Thomas the Rhymer.

Legendary figures

Many prominent people in Scotland's history have acquired legendary status, some because of their bravery, others because of infamous deeds, others still because of the strange or miraculous things that they were said to have done or said. The stories that are told about people such as these continue to intrigue and entertain. Rob Roy is remembered as Scotland's answer to Robin Hood and the story Bruce's encounter with the spider is solemnly told as encouragement to restless and impatient schoolchildren. John Graham of Claverhouse has acquired an ambiguous reputation, part hero, part horror, while the more obscure prophecies of the Brahan Seer are still interpreted and re-interpreted as the world changes and history moves on.

ROB ROY MACGREGOR AND MACALPINE OF CLAN GRANT

Rob Roy was born in Buchananan, Stirlingshire, in 1671, the third son of Donald Glas, a chief of the clan MacGregor. He fought at the Battle of Killiecrankie when he was only eighteen years old and continued to support the Jacobite cause for the rest of his life. After his marriage in 1693, he lived by Loch Lomond for more than ten years and earned his living as a cattle trader. He also took part in protection schemes, whereby Lowland cattle owners paid him and his people money to ensure the safekeeping of their cattle from cattle raiders. The Marquis of Montrose invested in Rob Roy's cattle trade, lending him large sums of money for purchases, but their relationship turned sour when one of the men in Rob Roy's employ disappeared with £1000 of Montrose's money. When Montrose demanded recompense, Rob Roy ignored him and was evicted from his lands on Loch Lomond.

In the years following his dispute with Montrose, Rob Roy led the life of an outlaw. He was charged with treason after leading his clan in the Jacobite rising in 1715, but escaped justice. He lived by protection schemes and cattle raiding, incurring the wrath of the wealthy, who suffered from his activities, and the gratitude of the poor, to whom he gave assistance. He was captured on more than two occasions, but managed to escape and although his enemies were numerous, he had no shortage of powerful allies to shelter him. Throughout all this time, he continued to hold the MacGregor clan together.

The exploits of Rob Roy became legendary. Undoubtedly he lived beyond the law, but his daring escapades, his skill with a broadsword (attributable in part, it is said, to his incredibly long arms), his support of the underdog and his loyalty to his clansmen earned him a reputation as a hero. The following story is only one of many that have been told about the bold MacGregor. It illustrates clearly some of the attributes for which he was remembered so fondly by so many.

MacAlpine of Clan Grant, Laird of Rothiemurchus, was in dispute with the chief of Clan Mackintosh. Mackintosh believed that the lands of Rothiemurchus rightfully belonged to him, and continually pressed his point with petty harassment. On this occasion, however, events had taken a more serious turn. Mackintosh had diverted the course of a stream running through MacAlpine's land so that it could power the wheel of a mill he had just built, and MacAlpine had objected, demanding that the mill be destroyed. Mackintosh's response was to threaten the Grants with attack, and Grant was now facing disaster, for his men were greatly outnumbered by the Mackintoshes. In desperation, he sent word to Rob Roy MacGregor that he needed his assistance. MacGregor was an ally of MacAlpine and had given his word that he would come to his aid in time of need.

The Mackintoshes were assembling and making preparations for their attack as MacAlpine waited anxiously in the Doune of Rothiemurchus for some sign that Rob Roy had responded to his plea. Finally, a familiar figure walked in, and greeted MacAlpine warmly. It was Rob Roy MacGregor, but he was alone. MacAlpine expressed his pleasure at seeing his old ally with some reserve. Where were Rob Roy's men? Seeing MacAlpine's concern, Rob Roy laid a reassuring hand on his shoulder. Then he summoned MacAlpine's piper and sent him out in front of the Doune, ordering him to play MacGregor's Gathering. No sooner had the piper begun to play than the members of Clan Gregor began to appear in groups of two or three from the cover of the trees nearby. The piper played on, and more and more armed men appeared until a force of more than one hundred of them stood there, fully armed and ready for battle. The sight of the MacGregors gathering was too much for the bold Mackintosh, and when he saw them assembled by the Doune of Rothiemurchus, he decided that prudence was the better part of valour and ordered his men to retreat.

The mill that had so offended MacAlpine was burned to the ground. Rob Roy then sent a letter to Mackintosh, warning him that any further harassment of MacAlpine would result in dire consequences. Unless Mackintosh left MacAlpine in peace, the MacGregors would return and destroy the Mackintosh lands with fire and sword. Then he took his men and left Rothiemurchus. He had fulfilled his pledge of support for the Grants, but he left them with the assurance that he would return again, if ever the need arose.

bruce and the spider

Robert the Bruce is remembered as one of Scotland's great heroes, both in history and in legend. One of the most popular stories about Robert the Bruce, and one which many schoolchildren are familiar with, concerns Bruce's encounter with a courageous and persistent spider, and the lesson he learned from the doughty little creature.

Robert the Bruce was in flight from the English. He had found a cave in which to seek refuge, and there he paused to regain his strength and to consider his future. The battle for Scotland's independence had seen so much bloodshed. After the terrible defeat at the Battle of Falkirk, William Wallace, inspiration to so many Scots, including Bruce, had been driven into flight. Now, after a cruel betrayal, he counted among the dead. Bruce himself was exhausted and ready to give up. As he lay back against the damp walls of the cave, lost in thought, he caught sight of a small movement out of the corner of his eye. A small spider was trying to spin a web from ceiling to wall, just at the entrance to the cave. Bruce watched in fascination as the spider spun a long, slender strand from an anchor point at the top of the cave mouth and swung it over to a lower point, on the wall. But just as the spider reached the second point, the start of the web came adrift from its anchorage. Undaunted, the spider crawled back to the starting-place and began the process again. Once again, the first strand had hardly spanned the corner of the cave mouth when it collapsed. But the spider did not give up. It went straight back to the beginning and set to work a third time. The weary warrior watched in growing admiration as the spider tried again, and again, to complete its task, each time failing at almost the same point. It must have tried six times or more, and with each attempt, Bruce found himself willing the little creature more and more to succeed. At last the spider's tenacity was rewarded and a fine silken thread stretched from roof to wall. Once the first thread was in place, it completed the rest of the web without any further difficulty.

Bruce closed his eyes in relief. Now he must rest. But he had learned a valuable lesson from the spider. He had to continue his struggle against the English oppressor. He could not let himself give up, for there was no victory in resignation. Bruce took up the sword again. In 1314, he finally led an army to victory against the English at the Battle of Bannockburn, which marked a turning point in Scotland's struggle for independence.

It is not clear either when, or where, the events in the story took place. Some people believe that the story dates from the winter of 1313, a few months before Bannockburn. Others believe that it has an earlier date, possibly 1306, after the Battle of Methven.

There are several sites that lay claim to being the location of the cave in which Bruce was inspired by the spider. One of them is not in Scotland, but in Ireland, on Rathlin Island. Rathlin Island is where Bruce sought refuge in 1306, not long after he had been crowned king of Scotland. The cave in question is only accessible by sea. Sites in Scotland include Bruce's Cave at Kilpatrick, Fleming in Dumfriesshire, King's Cave on Jura, Uamh-na-Righ at Craigruie near Balquidder and King's Cave at Drumadoon on Arran.

It may be that none of these caves was ever visited by Robert the Bruce. The legend may be no more than a charming fiction, created after Bruce's death. But over the years, many a child has taken inspiration from this story and its hero, and the moral that the story reveals has been gladly learned and taken to heart: If at first you don't succeed, try, try and try again.

Claverhouse warned

John Graham of Claverhouse, Viscount Dundee, was a remarkable man. He was a brave and loyal soldier who was prepared to fight for what he believed in. His courage was an inspiration to fellow supporters of the Jacobite cause in the seventeenth century and the role that he played in the first Jacobite rising, however brief, is remembered in history, legend and song. As far as the history of the Jacobite risings is concerned, Claverhouse was 'Bonnie Dundee', staunch supporter of the House of Stewart who led his men to victory at Killiecrankie, sacrificing his own life in doing so. But while Claverhouse was a powerful ally, he was also a fearsome foe, and his exploits in hunting down

Scottish Covenanters in the south west of Scotland had earned him a different title – 'Bluidy Clavers'. He could be ruthless and cruel to such an extent that some said he was a servant of the Devil, and that it was no ordinary bullet that had killed him at Killiecrankie but a silver one – the only effective weapon against the Devil's own.

Before the Battle of Killiecrankie, it is said that Claverhouse had a grim visitation from the realms of the dead. He was lying resting in his tent when the figure of a man appeared before him. The apparition was soaked in blood that was oozing from a bullet wound in his head. He pointed at Claverhouse, saying 'Remember Brown of Priesthill!' The figure must have struck fear into the heart of Claverhouse, for Brown of Priesthill was a martyr to the Covenanting cause, one of the many whom Claverhouse had hunted down. When Brown had been captured, he had refused to offer prayers for the king and as punishment, he had been condemned to a summary execution by a firing squad of Claverhouse's men. But he had shown extraordinary courage and resolve, even in the face of death, and instead of begging for mercy, had knelt calmly down to say his own prayers for his wife and family. When given the command to fire, Claverhouse's men had hesitated, unnerved by Brown's courage and conviction. Claverhouse himself had drawn his pistol and cold-bloodedly fired the fatal shot as Brown's wife looked on.

When it had said all it wanted to say, the gruesome spectre of Brown of Priesthill disappeared. Claverhouse at once called on the soldiers guarding his tent and asked if they had seen anything or anyone. He quizzed them carefully, to check that their attention had not wandered, wondering at the same time whether someone might be playing a trick on him. But all was quiet in the camp, and there seemed to be no rational explanation for the grim apparition's appearance. We can only imagine the sort of thoughts that were running through Claverhouse's mind as he tried to settle to sleep in preparation for the battle the next day.

The Highland forces under Claverhouse's command were outnumbered three to one by the government troops, and although the Highlanders had the advantage of the high ground there were gaps in their lines. Claverhouse waited until early evening, when the sun was beginning to go down, before he gave his men the order to advance. When they did so, it was with immense courage, and at terrible cost. They charged on relentlessly amidst a hail of enemy bullets until they were within feet of the English, then casting aside their muskets, they drew their broadswords and set about the enemy in hand to hand combat. The brute force, grim determination and speed with which the Highlanders carried out their assault took their toll on the enemy forces, and soon victory for the Jacobites was in sight. Claverhouse was riding into the thick of it, urging his men on, when a bullet struck him in the chest and he fell dying from his horse. Was his last thought of victory? Or was it the realisation that Brown's ghostly visitation the night before had been a grim warning of the fate that awaited him at Killiecrankie?

the brahan seer

On Chanonry Point near Fortrose stands a stone which was erected in memory of Scotland's most famous prophet, the Brahan Seer. It was at this spot that he is believed to have been executed on the orders of Isabella, wife of the third Earl of Seaforth. The Brahan Seer was Kenneth Mackenzie, or Coinneach Odhar, and he lived in Scotland in the seventeenth century. Little is known about his early life, but it is thought that he was born on the Isle of Lewis and that he moved to the mainland to seek work as a labourer on the Seaforth estates when he reached adulthood. Coinneach Odhar had the gift of second sight, and with the aid of a magical white seeing-stone that he was given as a young child, he could predict events far into the future. Many of his predictions have already come true, some with startling accuracy. Coinneach Odhar foresaw the Battle of Culloden. He also predicted the building of the Caledonian Canal. The words with which the Brahan Seer foretold the coming of the Highland clearances make sobering reading:

> There is a day coming when the jaw-bone of the big sheep will put the plough into the rafters and no man will drive cattle through Kintail. The sheep will become so numerous that the bleating of one shall be heard by another from Lochalsh to Kintail. You will not see it, but your children's children will see it when they are forced to flee before the march of the great white army, and the mountains will see it as I am seeing it now.

In 1851, in the ruins of Fairburn Tower, another of the Brahan Seer's predictions was fulfilled in a most amusing manner. The seer had foretold the end of the family line of the Mackenzies of Fairburn, in Ross-shire, and it had come to pass, in 1850, when Sir Alexander Mackenzie died without an heir. But there was another part of the seer's prophecy that was a little stranger than the rest:

The great castle of Fairburn will become uninhabited and forgotten and a cow will give birth to a calf in the uppermost chamber of the tower.

Fairburn Tower had been left uninhabited for a number of years. It was now in a semi-ruinous state and had been commandeered by a local farmer, who used it as a hay-store. One of the farmer's cattle, heavily pregnant, followed a trail of hay that had been dropped on the path leading to the tower, entered, and somehow managed to make her way right to the top. There she stuck, too large to be turned and led down, until she had been safely delivered of her calf. The Brahan Seer's prophecy was well known in the district and consequently, the cow became something of a celebrity during her confinement.

The most chilling prophecy of the Brahan Seer was a curse upon the family that employed him, the Mackenzies of Seaforth. Coinneach Odhar had served the family for several years. The countess knew of her servant's uncanny ability to see things beyond the vision of other people, and one day she asked him to give her news of her husband, the Earl of Seaforth, who was in France attending to business matters, or so she thought. Coinneach Odhar's answer was fairly non-committal. He simply told the countess that her husband was fit and well, and enjoying Paris society. But the countess pressed him for further information, and eventually, he reluctantly told her that the Earl was keeping company with another woman. The Countess was enraged by the news and vented her anger on the messenger. She gave the order fo Coinneach Odhar to be taken from his home to Fortrose, to be tried for witchcraft. He was found guilty, condemned to death, and was taken to Chanonry point where he was burned in a tar barrel. The curse that the Brahan Seer uttered just before he died was as follows:

I see far into the future, where lies the doom of Seaforth. Mackenzie to Mackenzie, Kintail to Kintail, Seaforth top Seaforth, all will end in extinction and sorrow. I see a chief, the last of his house, and he is both deaf and dumb. He will be father to four fine sons, but he will follow them all to the grave. He will live in sorrow and die in mourning, knowing that the honours of his line are extinguished forever and that no future chief of the clan Mackenzie shall ever again rule in Kintail. Lamenting the last of his sons, he shall sink in sorrow to the tomb and the last of his possessions shall be inherited by a white-coifed widow from the east, and she will kill her own sister. As a sign that these things are coming to pass, there will be four great lairds in the days of the last Seaforth. Gairloch shall be hare-lipped; Chisholm shall be buck-toothed, Grant shall be a stammerer and Raasay an idiot. These four chiefs shall be allies and neighbours of the last Seaforth and when he looks around him and sees them, he will know that his sons are doomed to die and that his broad lands shall pass to strangers and his race come to an end.

In the early decades of the nineteenth century, every element of this curse was fulfilled, one after another. The man who was doomed to be the last Earl of Seaforth was Francis Humberston Mackenzie. Among his contemporaries were four lairds, Gairloch, Chisholm, Grant and Raasay, who were afflicted in the manner that the seer had foretold. The earl was not born deaf, but lost his hearing as a result of childhood illness. His deafness affected him more severely in his declining years. He became more and more reluctant to speak as he grew older, and eventually resorted to communicating by writing. The earl had four sons and six daughters, and all his sons predeceased him. The oldest son died in infancy. The last to die was the third-born, who died one year before his father.

When the earl died in 1815, the male line died with him. The estate, or what was left of it, for much of it had been sold in the earl's lifetime, passed to the eldest of his six daughters, Mary. Mary had married Admiral Hood and was living in India, but when Hood died, she returned to Brahan, wearing the traditional Indian white mourning hood. She was the 'white-coifed widow from the east'. The estates of the Seaforth Mackenzies diminished piece by piece as more and more lands were sold off.

A monument by the roadside, not far to the west of Brahan House, marks the spot where the final element of the Brahan Seer's prophecy was fulfilled. It was erected in memory of Lady Caroline, Mary's sister. Caroline was riding in a carriage driven by Mary when the ponies bolted and Mary lost control. The carriage crashed and Caroline was thrown out onto the road. Mary survived the accident, but Caroline died from the injuries she received. The accident happened in 1823, almost one hundred and fifty years after the terrible curse had been pronounced.

The monument stands as a chilling reminder of how the fate of one family was crushed by the words of one man.

celtic myths of heroes and fair maids

deirdre of the sorrows

This story, like many of the tales in this book, can be found in a number of different versions. Its origins are in Ireland but like many Celtic myths, it has been absorbed into Scottish story-telling with variations here and there and has been for many years accepted as a Scottish myth as much as it is an Irish one.

According to some versions of the story, Deirdre was born and brought up in Scotland. But more commonly, it is said that she was born in Ireland.

Deirdre was the daughter of an elderly Irish bard. The bard and his wife had been married for many years and they thought that the marriage was destined to be childless. Then one day they were visited by a seer, who told them that soon the bard's wife would give birth to a daughter, who would be the cause of terrible bloodshed in Erin. Three great heroes of Erin would lose their lives on account of the child that was to be born, and great sorrow and confusion would follow.

The couple were angry at the soothsayer's words, and turned him out of the house. What he was telling them was impossible. Their time for having children was long gone. The soothsayer was no more than a wicked liar, spreading falsehoods and unhappiness. But as the weeks went by, it became clear that the bard's wife had indeed become pregnant, and when the child was born, and the couple saw that it was a daughter, they cast their minds back to the soothsayer's prediction, and their hearts were filled with dread. They decided that the child must be kept safe somewhere, far from the company of others. If she was kept apart from society then surely neither she, nor anyone else, could come to any harm. The child, whom they had called Deirdre, was handed over to a midwife to look after, and a small dwelling-place was found for the two to live in, deep in the countryside where no-one might find them.

Deirdre grew stronger and more beautiful every day in the care of the midwife. The years passed and she moved from childhood into adolescence. Time seemed to fly, and soon she was approaching womanhood, but although Deirdre knew all that there was to know about the creatures and wild flowers of the countryside, she knew nothing of what it was like to live in the company of men, and was not wise in the ways of the world.

One night a hunter who had lost his way in the darkness came knocking at the cottage door. The midwife, ever mindful of her duty to protect her child from the outside world, warned Deirdre not to answer, but Deirdre ignored her. She opened the door and welcomed the man in to warm himself by the fire. As soon as the hunter saw Deirdre, he realised that this was a maiden so lovely that all the heroes of Erin would fall for her charms, if only they could see her. The midwife saw the look in the visitor's eyes and knew that he could bring trouble to her door. When the hunter wondered aloud why the midwife was keeping such a beautiful girl hidden away when she could have her choice of the finest men in the country, the midwife angrily dismissed his questions.

She wanted him out of her house. She made it quite clear to him that his presence was not welcome and sent him on his way.

The hunter left, but the picture of Deirdre stayed in his mind's eye. She was so beautiful that he felt sure that even the king of Erin, Conachar himself, would be proud to take her as his wife. And if the hunter could effect an introduction between the two, he might be suitably rewarded. With this in mind, the hunter made his way to the royal palace and asked for an audience with the king, and just as he had hoped, King Conachar was intrigued to hear his news. Conachar expressed his wish to see the mysterious maiden living in isolation in the depths of the countryside, and he offered handsome sum of money in return for the hunter's services as a guide, to take him to Deirdre.

When the king's company came knocking at the door of the cottage demanding admittance, the midwife knew she had no choice but to let them in. As soon as Conachar laid eyes on Deirdre, he fell in love with her. But he could see that although she was old enough in years for marriage, she was still young in her heart and very naïve. He declared that she must come back with him to the royal palace where she would live for a year before becoming his wife. The midwife's tearful protestations went unheeded as arrangements were made for Deirdre to leave her forever.

Months passed, and with every passing day, Deirdre grew more beautiful and more assured. Blessed with the gift of natural grace, she found it easy to adopt the elegant manners of royal society. And dressed in fine silk and velvet gowns, she was the loveliest of all the women that had been seen in the court of the king. She had the company of several female attendants for conversation and entertainment, and they guided her gently towards her future life as queen. Deirdre had been accustomed to a solitary existence for all of her early years, but she revelled in the companionship and laughter that her new life brought her.

One day, as Deirdre and her attendants were out walking, they caught sight of three riders in the distance. The riders drew nearer and Deirdre saw three dark-haired young men, strikingly handsome, tall and athletic. One of the riders was taller than the other two by a head, and of the three, he was by far the most handsome.

Deirdre lost all interest in walking.

'Who are these men?' she asked of her companions. She asked about all of them, but her eyes had become fixed on the tallest one.

'They are brothers, the sons of Uisne,' replied one woman. 'That one is Aillean, and next to him is Ardan. The third one,' she said, pointing to the tallest and most handsome, 'is Naois'.

'Let us ask them to stop, for I would like to speak to them,' said Deirdre. But her attendants looked at her, and saw what was in her eyes, and shook their heads. 'Let them be on their way,' they said, 'and remember that you are betrothed to the king.'

Deirdre paid no heed to their words of warning. She did not know it, for she had never learnt what these feelings meant, but she was falling in love with Naois, and as her heart was captured by the sight of him, so her ears became deaf to her companions' advice. As the riders passed by, she called out his name.

'Naois! Naois!'

'Who called my name?' said Naois.

The brothers of Naois had seen Deirdre. They knew she was betrothed to Conachar.

'No-one called your name,' they said. 'It was the cries of the birds that you heard.'

Deirdre called his name again. ' Naois! Naois! Wait for me!' she cried. 'Do not leave me here!'

Naois could not ignore Deirdre's call this time, for he had heard her words, loud and clear. He pulled his horse around to look at Deirdre, and she ran up to him and embraced him. Then she kissed his lips, and his heart was lost.

Naois knew that there was no future for them in Erin, for when the king heard what he had done, he would hunt him down to take his revenge. He took Deirdre up behind him on his horse and rode away, with his brothers following. They did not stop until they reached the coast, where they found a boat to sail to Scotland. They travelled to Loch Etive in Argyll, where they settled down to live together.

Conachar heard about Deirdre and the sons of Uisne, and he discovered where they were living, but he did not follow them. He waited for almost a year, until the day on which Deirdre was supposed to have married him, then he sent an envoy across the sea to Argyll, inviting Naois, Deirdre, Aillean and Ardan to a banquet, with assurances that he did so with friendly intent.

When Deirdre heard of Conachar's invitation, she begged Naois to refuse. She saw deceit and treachery behind the congenial words of Conachar's envoy, and feared for the lives of Naois and his brothers. But the three young heroes would not be accused of cowardice and were determined to go. If Conachar turned on them, they felt sure that they could count on the support of loyal friends. And so the matter was decided and Deirdre and the sons of Uisne set sail, back to the country of their birth.

Conachar had soldiers ready, waiting for their arrival. The night after Deirdre, Naois and his brothers arrived in Erin, they were attacked by Conachar's men. They were outnumbered several times over, but fought bravely and slew every one of their assailants. Word reached Conachar that his plan had failed, and he sent more men the next day. The attackers came in waves, and Naois and his brothers fought all day against them, hoping all the time that someone would come to their aid before their strength was gone. But as the hours passed and no help came, they realised that they could wait no longer and fled.

King Conachar heard that Deirdre and the sons of Uisne were escaping and grew angrier than ever. Now he called upon a Druid to use his magic to stop them leaving the country. Naois took Deirdre on his shoulders and led the retreat, heading with his brothers towards the sea, but they did not get far. The Druid cast his first spell and at once a forest, dense, dark and almost impassable, grew up around the fugitives. The sons of Uisne fought to make a passage through the thick, tangled undergrowth and at last, found their way out of the forest. Then the Druid cast a second spell, and caused the sea to flood the land beyond the forest. Waist-deep in icy water, the sons of Uisne struggled on without stopping, determined to reach the place where their ship lay waiting for them. When he saw that he had still not beaten them the Druid used his magic a third time and all at once it was winter. As the temperature dropped, the flood waters turned into a jagged sea of ice. Naois was still not ready to give up. He pleaded with his brothers to carry on. But Aillean and Ardan were already exhausted and now the cold was so fierce that they could not bear it. They sank down upon the ice, motionless. Naois looked on in anguish as his two brave, beloved brothers died, one after the other, on the frozen floodwaters.

Naois seemed to shrink with the pain of losing his brothers. His despair drained the last of the strength from his body, and his will to live faded away. Deirdre cried out to him to keep on moving, but he could not hear her words. He fell, close to the place where his brothers lay.

When Conachar was satisfied that Naois was dead, he made the Druid cast another spell, and the ice melted and the flood waters receded. Deirdre was left standing alone, with the bodies of her lover and his brothers lying on the grass beside her.

Conachar rejoiced when he heard that the sons of Uisne were dead, and that Deirdre was still alive. He sent men to dig a grave for the three brothers, and ordered that Deirdre be brought back to him. But when Deidre saw the body of Naois lying in the newly dug grave, she knew that she could not live without him. She lay down beside him and closed her eyes. Conachar would not get his bride back. Deirdre of the Sorrows had gone with the sons of Uisne.

diarmid and grainne

Finn, chief of the Fians, had a nephew, named Diarmid. Diarmid was a hero with a reputation for wisdom and courage almost as great as that of his uncle. He was also extraordinarily handsome. He was born with a special mark on the side of his forehead, and any woman who caught sight of the mark was destined to fall hopelessly in love with him. In order to spare himself from unwanted attentions, he had a helmet specially made to conceal the mark, and he rarely took it off. Finn loved Diarmid as a father loves a son.

When Finn had reached an age when his thoughts turned to marriage, he looked around to find a woman who was both beautiful and clever. Beauty Finn could see as well as any man, but wisdom must be judged in other ways, and so he asked the same questions of every woman who was brought before him.

What is hotter than fire?

What is quicker than the wind?

What is the best jewel?

What is blacker than a raven?

When Grainne, daughter of Cormac, appeared before him, Finn saw at once that she was beautiful. And when he set her the task of answering his questions, he learned that she was quick-witted too. Of all the women whom Finn had challenged in this way, she alone gave answers that satisfied him.

'What is hotter than fire?' he asked her.

'Why, a woman's reasoning between two men,' Grainne replied.

'And what is quicker than the wind?'

'A woman's thought between two men is far quicker than the wind,' she said.

'What is the best jewel?' Finn said.

'A knife is the most precious jewel one can possess,' she answered.

'And what is blacker than a raven?'

'No raven is as black as death.'

And so Finn found his wife.

The wedding celebrations went on for many days, and Diarmid took part in them gladly. Never before in the history of Erin had there been such feasting and drinking. But although Diarmid laughed and danced, ate and drank as much as any other man in the place, he made sure that his helmet remained firmly fixed on his head, keeping his birthmark well hidden from the sight of any woman.

As the celebrations were drawing to a close, some drunken revellers let the hunting dogs into the banqueting hall. No sooner had the dogs caught sight of the remnants of the feast, than they began to compete for bones and scraps of meat. Before long, a savage fight had broken out between them. Diarmid caught sight of the affray and moved in to separate the dogs, but they were strong brutes. In the struggle to prize them apart, his helmet was knocked from his head and fell to the floor. As he bent to retrieve it, Diarmid saw Grainne out of the corner of his eye. He could tell from the look that she gave him that she had caught sight of the birthmark. Although newly married to his uncle, Grainne's affections had turned to Diarmid and she had fallen passionately in love with him.

Diarmid swiftly withdrew from the banqueting hall, hoping to escape before it was too late. But Grainne saw him leaving. She followed him, cornered him in a darkened passageway and begged him to take her away with him. Her passion made her lose all sense of caution and she grasped him round the shoulders and pulled his body close to her. Diarmid resisted her advances, but already he could feel his resolve was weakening. He struggled from her arms, protesting his loyalty to Finn, and turned away. He ran to his apartments to gather his belongings. Then he vanished into the night.

Diarmid found shelter in a hunter's bothy in the woods. He hoped to rest there for the night before moving on at first light. He knew he could no longer stay in the same place as his uncle's wife. But he had hardly laid his head down to sleep when the door opened and Grainne came in, dressed in flimsy clothing, and looking more alluring than he had ever seen her before. This time Diarmid could not resist her charms. He pulled her down beside him and they spent the night entwined in each other's arms.

The two lovers knew that they had to flee, for as soon as Finn discovered their treachery, he would come after them. Before the first light of dawn began to filter through the trees, Diarmid and Grainne had abandoned the bothy and were heading for the coast. They sailed across to Kintyre, and then travelled from place to place, over the mainland and from one island to the next. They dare not rest in one place for any length of time, for they knew that if they did, Finn's men would find them.

Time passed, and Finn had almost given up his nephew for dead. Then it so happened that he crossed the sea from Ireland to take part in a boar hunt, and he came face to face with Diarmid in Glen Eilg.

Finn was now faced with a terrible dilemma. As long as Diarmid was out of sight, Finn's intentions towards him had been murderous. But now, with Diarmid before him, Finn remembered that this was the child to whom his sister had given birth, the boy whom he also loved like a son. He had not the heart to kill him in cold blood. Instead, he challenged Diarmid to kill the great boar, hoping, perhaps, that the boar would mete out the punishment his nephew so richly deserved.

The hunting party moved on, with Diarmid at the head. They tracked the beast for miles until at last they had it cornered in a rocky gully. Finn watched as Diarmid went in for the kill. The boar was far bigger than he was, and as it charged it looked set to knock the young hero off his feet. Diarmid braced himself, spear poised, not a tremor in the arm that held it. His two hunting dogs stood in front of their master, snarling and yelping. With a great roar, the boar tossed the dogs to the side with its tusks as if they weighed no more than a feather. Its feet carved great divots out of the ground as it thundered on towards Diarmid's spear, but still Diarmid did not move. When the boar was within feet of the young hunter, it lowered its head, ready to gore him with its great tusks, and the eyes of man and beast met. Diarmid thrust his spear with all his strength into the boar's chest. With a great cry of rage and pain it collapsed at his feet.

Finn looked on with pride and despair. Diarmid had shown tremendous courage, but Finn still could not forgive him for taking Grainne. He did not want to be the one to take his nephew's life and yet Diarmid's death was the only thing that would satisfy his need for revenge. Then Finn remembered that the boar's spines were poisonous, a fact of which Diarmid was not aware.

'How big is the beast?' he wondered aloud. 'And who will measure it?'

Diarmid at once jumped onto the boar and walked along the length of it from head to tail to measure it in steps.

'Surely it is longer than that,' said Finn, when he heard how big the boar was. 'Measure it again!'

And so Diarmid turned, and started walking back from the boar's tail towards its head, against the lie of the spines. He took one or two steps, then one of the spines sank into his bare foot. He fell to the ground in agony as the deadly poison entered his bloodstream and extinguished his life. With great sorrow in his heart, Finn saw that at last he had been avenged for the theft of his wife.

Clan Campbell claimed descent from Diarmid O Dubhne. On the clan crest is a boar's head, representing the beast that caused the death of the progenitor of the Campbells.

finn saves the children of the big young hero and finds bran

Finn and his men were resting after a day's hunting, sitting on a green knoll, warmed by the sun and sheltered from the wind. Finn looked towards the sea and saw a ship sailing into the cove below them. A Big Young Hero leapt ashore and dragged the ship onto the grass, and bounded up the hillside towards Finn and his men. He greeted Finn, and Finn asked him why he had come. The Hero said that he had sailed through storms night and day to find Finn, because he had lost his children and he knew that no other man could save them but Finn, king of the Fians. He laid upon Finn a vow to follow him. Then he turned away back down the hill, pushed his ship out to sea, and sailed away.

Finn knew he had to fulfil the vow, but did not know how to do it. He left his men and descended to the shore, but could follow the Big Young Hero no further. Then he saw seven men walking towards him. He asked the men who they were, and what they were good at. The first said he was a Carpenter and could build a great ship with three strokes of his axe. The second said he was a Tracker, and could track wild duck far over the sea. The third man was a Gripper and said that he never let go of what he held onto, even if his arms came away from his shoulders. The fourth man, a Climber, said he would climb a silken thread to the stars if it could be cast so far. The fifth man told Finn he was a Thief, so skilful that he could steal an egg from a heron while her eyes were upon him. The sixth man told Finn he was a Listener, who could hear what people were saying at the furthest ends of the earth, and the seventh said he was a Marksman, capable of hitting an egg as far up in the sky as a bow could shoot an arrow. Hearing these things, Finn was satisfied that the seven men were good enough for his company.

He spoke to the Carpenter first. 'Prove yourself!' The Carpenter found an alder stock nearby and gave it three mighty blows with his axe. As he had promised, he had made a fine strong ship. Finn and the seven men put the ship out so sea. Then Finn told the Tracker to go to the bow of the ship, to guide him as he steered the ship towards the place where the Big Young Hero had gone. They sailed on for many hours until night was drawing in, and they could see land ahead. They landed the ship, and saw the Big Young Hero coming down towards them from a house on the hill. Finn was angry with the Big Young Hero for leaving him without means of following, but the Big Young Hero soothed his anger, and told Finn he had sent the company of seven men to help him. They went to the house of the Big Young Hero and he made them welcome with plenty of food and drink. Then he told them what had happened to him.

'Six years ago, my wife gave birth to a child,' he said, 'but as soon as the child was born a great hand came down the chimney and took the child away. Three years later, my wife had another child and the same thing happened. Tonight, my wife will give birth again, and the same thing will happen again. You are the only one who can save my children for me.'

The seven men were tired and Finn told them to lie down and sleep, while he kept watch. He kept a bar of iron in the fire, and whenever sleep began to overcome him, he burned his hand with the iron bar to keep himself awake. In the middle of the night the child was born, and at once a great Hand came in at the chimney. Finn woke the Gripper. The Gripper pulled on the hand and brought it in up to the elbow. Then the hand pulled back and the Gripper was almost pulled out of the chimney. To and fro the Gripper and the Hand pulled, this way and that. Then the Gripper gave one final mighty tug and tore the hand from its shoulder. The Gripper fell to the floor with the hand beside him, but his struggle was in vain. The giant outside put his other hand down the chimney and, cupping the newborn child in his palm, took it away.

Finn would not give up. The next morning, before the light of dawn, he set out in his ship with the seven men to find the hand, the Tracker guiding their course. They sailed for many hours until they came to a great black rock in the middle of the sea. At the very top of the rock was a castle, thatched in eel-skins. There were no windows and no doors to be seen, and the castle walls and roof were steep and slippery, so they could see no way in. But the Climber believed he could get to the castle roof, and asked to prove his worth. He scaled the walls in no time at all and found the door in the roof of the castle. He looked in to see what was there, then he came down again to tell what he had seen. He told Finn that a Giant lay sleeping inside, with a baby in the palm of his hand. Two children were playing on the floor with golden shinties and a silver ball, and by the fire, a great deerhound bitch lay suckling two pups.

Now was the time for the Thief to prove himself. The Climber carried the Thief on his back up onto the castle roof, and he went inside. First, he took the baby from the giant's cupped hand, and passed it out. Then he passed out the other two children, the golden shinties and the silver ball. He stole the silken sheet that covered the giant as he slept and passed it out. Last, he took the two pups from the deerhound and passed them out before coming out himself. When the children and the stolen goods were aboard the ship, Finn and his men set sail. But they had not gone far, when the Listener gave the alarm. 'I hear the giant waking,' he said, 'and he is sending the Bitch after us!'

Finn looked back and saw the great dog making her way towards them, red-hot sparks lighting the water as she ploughed her course through the waves. Finn's men were afraid, and did not know what to do. 'Throw out one of the pups', he said. 'The Bitch will not let it drown. She will take it back to shore to save it.' The men threw one of the pups overboard, and it was just as Finn said. The Bitch took the pup and swam back to shore with it. Then the Listener gave them a second warning.

'The giant is trying to send the Bitch after us again, but she will not go,' he said, 'and he is saying he will come after us himself!' Once again, Finn's men were frightened, and did not know what to do. They thought that the giant could not be slain. But Finn knew a secret about the giant. He had a vulnerable spot, a mole on the palm of his hand, and only this kept him from being immortal. Finn told the Marksman what he knew. 'If I can see the blemish,' said the Marksman, 'I can surely hit it with my arrow.'

The giant strode through the waves towards the ship and Finn and his men waited fearfully. As the giant reached the stern of the ship, he reached out to take hold of the mast. He opened his hand and the Marksman saw the mole and took aim. The arrow flew straight and true to the vulnerable spot and the giant fell dead into the sea. With nothing to fear, Finn and his men sailed back to the castle, where the Thief took back the pup they had thrown overboard. Then they sailed to the place where the Big Young Hero lived and returned his children to him. The Big Young Hero was overjoyed.

'What can I give you as a reward?' he said to Finn.

'Only one thing,' said Finn, 'and that is my choice of the two pups we took from the castle.'

Finn would take no more, whatever the Big Young Hero offered, and so it was that Finn took one dog, which he named Bran, and the Big Young Hero got the other, and it became known as the Grey Dog. Then the Big Young Hero invited Finn and his men to a feast, and their celebrations continued for a year and a day.

giant Lore

The countryside of Scotland is quieter now, for most of the giants are dead, or slumbering beneath the hills on which they used to sit. But in times gone by, the sound of their battles echoed across the glens and the noise made by the missiles that they threw at one another across lochs and estuaries here and there sent fishermen fleeing to the safety of the shores in their boats. These battles were a favourite form of entertainment for the giants. Two rivals, sitting on the tops of adjoining hills, or perched on promontories at either side of a bay, would take it in turns to fling their weapons – boulders, hammers, or great pickaxes – at one another. Sometimes one island-dwelling giant would pick a fight with another, living on another island near to him, and great stones would be hurled across the sea between the two. The giants did little damage to each other, for we are told that the accuracy with which they aimed these missiles left much to be desired.

All over Scotland lies a litter of stones that are said to have been left where they fell, after being hurled by one giant at another. Two great boulders, one white and one black, were left on opposite shores of Loch Ness after a feud between two giants who lived near there ended in stalemate. Another giant who lived in Kintail, once tried to hit a rival who lived across the water in Skye. He missed, and the boulder that he flung crashed to the ground near Portree. There are giants' boulders on the east coast and the west, on the shores of the Cromarty

Firth and in the Hebrides, in the Grampians, the Cairngorms, the hills of Fife and the Scottish Borders. On Law Hill, by Dundee, the 'De'il's Stane' can be found. It is said that it was thrown across the Tay by a giant from Norman's Law at his rival on Law Hill, but fell short of its mark. At Ben Ledi, overlooking the town of Callander, a more amicable contest took place between a number of giants. A giant who was given the name of Samson lived there, and believing that he was the strongest of all, he challenged all comers to a shot-putting contest. The 'shot' was a boulder of enormous size, which they took it in turns to throw from the summit of Ben Ledi. 'Samson's putting-stone' lies where he last flung it, on the east side of the Ben.

The giants could be a terrible torment to humans, and they were notoriously hard to kill. Traditionally, as the story of Finn and the Big Young Hero has already illustrated, they could be slain if their vulnerable spot – usually described as a mole – could be found. Otherwise, as the story of Finlay and the Giants on page 126 tells us, it took a combination of perseverance, brute strength, ingenuity and magic to kill them.

the morvern giant

Long ago, there lived a great giant in Morvern, which is on the west coast of Argyll, between Loch Linnhe and Loch Sunart. Across the sea from Morven, on the Isle of Mull, lived several more giants, whom the Morvern giant disliked intensely. He would often amuse himself by tossing boulders at them, across the Sound of Mull.

He was bigger and stronger than any of the Mull giants, and he succeeded in causing one or two of them serious injury, much to his delight. The Morvern giant could pick up a cow or a bullock with one hand, and it made a fine meal for him. The sea provided another source of food for the giant, but of course, there was not a fish big enough to satisfy his appetite. When he went fishing, he was looking for a much bigger catch. His fishing rod was made from a tall, straight, silver birch tree, from which he had torn all the branches and roots. His line had been stolen from some fishermen, and it was the longest, strongest rope that they had. For a hook, the giant used an anchor. He had picked it up from the bottom of the harbour and snapped the rope that tied it to its ship. The ship had floated out into the sea in the middle of the night and had never been seen again.

The giant would sit on a hillock by the water at the Point of Ardnamurchan, and cast his great hook and line far out to sea. Then one after another, he would haul great whales in to shore, roaring with laughter as they thudded onto the beach.

The giant was also a thief, and one day he stole some treasure from the king of Ardnamurchan. He did not need to sneak past the guards. He did not have to creep in under cover of darkness. He simply stuck his hand down a chimney and helped himself to all the gold and silver that was lying in the room below.

The king and his men gave chase, which was a very brave thing to do, considering the size and strength of the thief. The giant was heading eastward from the Point of Ardnamurchan, trudging along the northern shore of Loch Sunart, heading for the end. The king and his men knew that when the giant got to the end of the loch, he would turn south and west again, heading for his home in Morvern, and so they got in a boat and crossed Loch Sunart from north to south in order to intercept him. The cries of the king as he urged on his oarsmen alerted the giant to his pursuers. He picked up a great boulder and lifted it high above his head. Then he threw it into the loch, making great waves that tossed the king's boat from side to side like a twig in a torrent. But the king's men would not give up. With tremendous courage and tenacity, they battled through the raging waters to the other side of the loch, just as the giant was making his way up the hillside towards his home.

Then the bravest warrior among the king's men called out to the giant, challenging him to stop and fight. The giant laughed, for he knew that he had the strength to crush every one of the king's men with his bare hands. He turned his face towards them, ready to answer the challenge with a scornful sneer.

But when the warrior who had shouted out the challenge looked at the giant's face, he saw that there was a red mole right in the middle of his forehead, and knew that this was his weak spot. He drew his bow and, swiftly and surely, shot an arrow at the giant's forehead, hitting him right in the middle of the blemish. With a crash that echoed all across the peninsula, the giant fell dead to the ground. The king's men gathered up the stolen treasure and loaded it onto their boat. Then they cut off the giant's head and rolled it down the hillside to the shore.

The weight of their load almost sank their boat as they sailed back over the loch to Ardnamurchan, with the triumphant giant slayer at the helm.

the tormented giantess

In Banffshire, in the north-east of Scotland, two great beings lived many years ago. Their lair was on a hill in Strathdown. One was male and the other female, and they lived as man and wife, but the giant was a terrible bully, and abused the giantess dreadfully. He quarrelled with her almost nightly, and when he became angry he beat her, he tore her hair and he kicked her. The sound of the blows that the landed upon his wife, and the terrible screams of pain and anger that the giantess let out as he hit her, shattered the peace of the countryside for miles around.

There was one man who found the noise of the giants' quarrels particularly disturbing. His name was James Gray, and he was a tenant farmer in Delnabo. Night after night, his family were kept awake by the sound of the thumping and screaming, and they were growing desperately weary. Eventually, Gray was driven to venture up the hill to see whether he might intervene in the dispute and bring some peace to his house. Halfway up, he met the giantess, slumped in a great heap on the hillside, weeping bitterly. She had just received another beating from her heartless husband, and he had thrown her out of the house. Gray felt sorry for her and furious with the brute who had left her so battered and bruised, but he was at a loss as to how he might help her, for he was no match for the giant's strength.

'If he has thrown you out, then why do you not take your chance and flee?' he said to the sobbing giantess. Although she was smaller than her husband, she towered above the farmer and her great tears splashed all about him and soaked his clothes.

'What would be the good of that when I know that in a few moments, he will come to drag me back?' she wailed. 'His greatest pleasure in life is causing me pain, and no matter how much I may beg him to show me some kindness, he is deaf to my pleas. I am helpless against him.'

'Then what can be done?' said Gray. 'If he will not listen to reason then there is nothing I can do. You know as well as I do that a man cannot kill a giant.'

There was no time for the giantess to reply, for just then they heard a thundering sound on the hillside above them, and the thump, thump, thump, of great footsteps approaching. The giant was coming after his wife. Gray turned and fled for the safety of his home.

The next night there was a loud thudding on his door. When Gray opened the door he found the giantess standing outside, waiting for him.

'What is it you want of me?' he said. 'I have already told you that there is nothing I can do. I am only a farmer. I cannot do battle with a giant!'

Then the giantess told him of the giant's weak spot. On the left side of his breast, she told him, was a mole, red in colour and about the size of a man's fist.

'If you can keep your hand steady and your aim true,' said the giantess, 'then we can be rid of the brute.'

The thought of confronting the giant made Gray's blood run cold, and at first he refused to help the giantess, but she wheedled and cajoled and at last he relented. He gathered up his bow and arrow, and climbed onto her shoulders. The giantess strode up the hill with her trembling burden, taking steps five times the length of a man's stride. She carried Gray as easily as if he were a new-born puppy. When they drew near to the giants' lair, she went on tiptoe, lest she disturb her sleeping husband, but the ground beneath her still shook with the weight of her feet. Carefully, she set James Gray down in front of the door and pointed.

'Draw your bow,' she said, 'and aim high.' Willing his hands to stop shaking with all his might, Gray did as he was told. Then the giantess let out a terrible shriek to wake the giant. The giant came crashing from his bed and threw the door open. His fury at the disturbance was plain to see, for his fists were so tightly clenched that his knuckles turned white, and the leathery skin on his forehead was creased into deep, angry furrows. His dark eyes glistened with rage and the heat from his breath sent clouds of steam puffing into the cold night air. Gray was ready to turn and run, but the giantess stopped him.

'There!' she cried, and pointed to a round, red mark on the giant's breast. 'There!'

Gray took aim, and fired. The giant roared as the arrow pierced his skin, right in the middle of the vulnerable spot. Then his flesh seemed to melt and he disappeared into thin air, and the arrow that had struck him fell to the ground with a clatter.

The grateful giantess rewarded James Gray well for his bravery. His family fed like royalty on the deer that she brought to his farm every week. And at night they slept soundly in their beds, for the terrible sound of her screaming was never heard again.

finlay and the giants

Finlay the hunter lived with his sister in a cottage at the

foot of a hill. Their relationship was not an amicable one. Finlay's sister resented him, and disliked his expectance that she should obey him. Every morning, Finlay set off at dawn with his hunting dogs, and every morning he gave the same instruction. 'Keep the window on the north side of the house closed.' Finlay said this for his sister's own good, because north was the direction from which evil came. But as soon as he had gone, his defiant sister opened the window on the north side of the house, for she had no wish to listen to his advice or to do as he said.

On his way back from hunting one day, Finlay caught sight of a tiny sheiling hidden in a hollow in the hillside. He had never noticed it before and was curious to find out who lived in it and so he went up to it and knocked on the door. An old woman answered and welcomed him inside. She was a wise widow, and shared the cottage with her daughter. She knew who Finlay was and had chilling words of warning for him.

'Be very careful when you go back home,' she told him. 'Your sister has fallen for the charms of the youngest of the giants who live on the hill. He is hiding in your cottage and waiting to kill you.'

Finlay thanked the old woman, and returned to his own cottage. His sister was waiting for him.

'See,' she said, 'I have collected fresh bedding for you to rest on tonight.' There was a great pile of straw in the corner. Underneath the straw, the giant was hiding, lying in wait. But Finlay had been well prepared for such a surprise by the words of the old widow. He went over to the fire, as if to warm himself. The he picked up the pot of water that was boiling on the fire and overturned it on the pile of straw. The giant leapt to his feet, crying with pain as the boiling water peeled the skin from his body, and Finlay's dogs pounced. The giant fled from the cottage, pursued by the snapping dogs. Finlay's sister ran out after him.

The next day, when his hunting was over, Finlay visited the old woman again and told her what had happened.

'You have done well,' she said, 'but you must prepare yourself for the giants' revenge. Save your strength for a great struggle and be glad that you have three strong dogs to help you.' Finlay returned to his house with a feeling of dread, and waited.

In the cave at the top of the hill, the giants debated which among them should be the one to avenge the youngest, and the hill shook with the sound of their arguing. At last it was agreed that the youngest giant's brother should go. He left the cave and strode down the hillside, his great feet churning up the rocky ground and an avalanche of boulders and mud fell down upon Finlay's cottage. Finlay waited, sure that he was facing death.

The giant was bigger and fiercer than his brother. He reached Finlay's cottage and thumped the door with his fist. The door snapped off its hinges and fell to the ground. Finlay fired at him once, twice, with his bow, but the arrows did not kill him. Then Finlay's dogs set upon the great hulk, tearing at his hair and snapping at his throat. Finlay took his sword and hacked at the giant's flesh with all his might, and finally the giant gave up the struggle and fell down dead. Finlay cut off the giant's head and kept it to show to the old widow the next day.

'You have done well,' she told him when he brought her the head, 'but you have more to do yet, and you will be even more glad of the help of your faithful hunting hounds. Another giant will come to your house tonight. He is the father of the two with whom you have done battle and he is bigger and more powerful than both of them. Have courage.'

Finlay returned to his cottage and waited with fear in his heart. Soon there came a terrible rumbling and thundering from outside. The third giant was making his way to the cottage and his footsteps were carving great chunks of rock from the hillside as he came. He reached the cottage door and roared out Finlay's name, demanding to be let in. Finlay did not open the door. So the giant thumped on the door with his fist, sending it flying off its hinges and into the middle of the cottage. The building shook.

Finlay was waiting with his bow and arrows. He shot at the giant once, twice, three times. The giant roared, but the arrows did not stop him. Finlay's dogs set upon the giant, tearing coarse strands of hair from his head and snapping and snarling at his throat, trying to get a grip. Finlay drew his sword and attacked, thrusting it to the hilt again and again into the giant's enormous belly and chest. After a tremendous struggle, the giant fell to the ground, the blood from his wounds making a great red pool on the cottage floor. Finlay cut off the head of the giant to show the widow the next day.

The widow was pleased with Finlay's achievement and greatly impressed with his bravery, but she told him that he was not done yet. The old woman, the Cailleach, would soon be coming to avenge her husband and sons.

'The Cailleach will not coming roaring and bellowing

down the hill as the men in her family did,' she warned Finlay. 'She will come in disguise and she will ask meekly and politely to be let into your home. Be warned. The Cailleach is the most dangerous of all of the giants, for she is full of tricks.'

Finlay went back to his cottage and waited. All was quiet outside. He could hear nothing except the sound of the wind in the trees. Then he heard a gentle knock at the door and a small voice coming from outside.

'I am cold and weary and in desperate need of shelter,' said the voice. 'Will you let me come in for a while to get warm?'

Finlay kept the door firmly shut. 'First you must promise that you will conduct yourself in a civil manner and that you will do me no harm.'

'As long as I am in your home, I promise that you will not be harmed,' said the voice. 'Now please, if you will, let me in, for the weather is growing colder by the second.'

Finlay opened the door and a small, old woman came in, her cheeks blue with the cold. She made to sit down at the fire, but Finlay's dogs sensed danger and prowled restlessly around her, growling and whimpering.

'Tie up your dogs,' said the old woman. 'They are frightening me.'

Finlay hesitated.

'Here,' said the old woman, holding out three red ribbons, 'tie them together with these ribbons.'

Finlay took the ribbons from the old woman, but remembered the wise widow's warning that the Cailleach was full of tricks. He ordered his dogs to lie down in the far corner of the room. He pretended to tie them up, but left them free to move at his command.

The old woman sat down by the fire and rubbed her hands together. As the flames warmed her hands, she began to grow.

'It seems as if you are getting bigger,' Finlay said to her.

'Ach, no,' she said. 'It is only that I was shrunken into myself with the cold.'

Finlay watched her warming herself by the fire a few moments longer. She grew bigger still.

'Old woman,' he said, 'you are still growing, and now you cannot deny it.'

The Cailleach now swelled to her full size and stood up to face Finlay. She was fearsomely ugly, with teeth like tusks protruding from her wizened mouth.

'You are afraid,' she snarled at him. 'You have good reason. You scalded my younger son, and you slew my older son and my husband. You may be sure that tonight I will kill you.'

Finlay reminded her of her promise not to harm him in his own home.

'A promise must be kept,' she replied, 'so you are safe in your house. But outside, I may do as I please.'

So saying, she took hold of Finlay and dragged him out of the cottage. Finlay called upon his dogs, and the three hounds set upon the Cailleach. The dogs tore at her hair and her clothing while Finlay wrestled with her. Back and forth they rolled upon the ground until Finlay struggled free from her grip and with a tremendous effort, pinned her to the ground. The Cailleach was powerless, with Finlay sitting on top of her and the three dogs each holding on to pieces of her with their teeth.

'Let me up,' she pleaded, 'and I will reward you richly. I will give you a chest full of gold and silver that lies in my cave.'

'That is mine by rights already,' said Finlay, 'for I have beaten you in combat.'

'I will give you a magic sword with a golden hilt that is hidden there,' the old woman wheedled. 'With this sword, you will be invincible against all foes.'

'Like the chest of gold and silver, the sword is mine already,' said Finlay, 'for I am the victor and these are my spoils.'

'Two more things can be yours, if only you will release me,' coaxed the Cailleach. 'There are two magic rods concealed at the back of my cave. If you touch a standing stone with one of them, it will turn into a warrior unlike any man that has ever lived. If you give him the sword with the golden hilt, he will have the strength and the wit to overcome all the enemies in the world. If you touch the warrior with the other rod, he will disappear. What else, Finlay, could you want of me?'

Finlay still did not let the Cailleach get up. 'These are all fine things,' he said to her, 'but I have won them already, fair and square. Have you nothing else to offer me as a bribe to let you go?'

The Cailleach shook her head wearily. Finlay took his sword and killed her where she lay. He cleaned and dressed his wounds and attended to his dogs, then he set off for the widow's house.

'I have killed the Cailleach,' he told her. 'It was a terrible struggle and I could not have done it without the help of my dogs.'

'Your dogs deserve the praise you give them,' said

the widow, 'but you also must be commended for your courage and strength.'

'I know there are rich rewards lying in the giants' cave,' said Finlay, 'but the youngest giant will still be there guarding the entrance and I do not know how I will get past him.'

'My daughter and I will come with you to the cave tomorrow night, and together we will overcome the giant,' the wise widow woman assured him. 'I have a magic wand which I can use against him.'

The next night the three of them set off up the hillside together. As they got close to the cave, they could hear the giant breathing in the darkness beyond the cave mouth. The widow told Finlay and her daughter what they must do. They gathered armfuls of dry heather and piled them up around the cave mouth. Then they set fire to the pile. The smoke poured into the cave and the giant's breathing became more laboured. Then he began to cough and splutter. He staggered to the mouth of the cave, with streaming eyes. Finlay drew his bow and prepared to shoot, but the widow held him back.

'If you hit him with an arrow, you will only wound him and make him more angry,' she warned him, 'and the smoke and the heat from the flames will hinder the dogs from helping you. Let me use my wand, and pray that I am lucky, for he has a sword in his hand and if I miss, he will kill me with a single blow.' With these words, the widow pounced at the giant and struck him on the head with her magic wand. The giant fell down dead.

Finlay and the widow stepped over the giant's body and entered the cave. At the back of the cave, they found Finlay's sister lying dead. Beside her was a chest full of gold and silver, just as the Cailleach had said. Hidden in another corner was the sword with the golden hilt and in another deep, dark, recess, the two magical rods. They carried them all out of the cave.

'These are your rewards,' said the wise widow, 'and you have earned them well. Every man, woman and child who lives in this district will sleep more soundly in their beds tonight, knowing that the giants have been slain.'

'I know that it was I who killed them,' said Finlay, 'but without your advice they would surely have killed me first. We must share the rewards between us.'

Finlay gave the chest of gold and silver to the widow and her daughter and kept the sword with the golden hilt and the two magic rods for himself. As they made their way back to the widow's house carrying their booty, they came across a standing stone. Finlay took one of the rods and struck the stone. The stone disappeared and in its place stood a strong and handsome warrior. Finlay gave the warrior the sword and watched as he grew in stature and strength. Here was a hero who could overcome any number of enemies, no matter how great. Then Finlay struck the warrior with the other rod. The warrior disappeared and the standing stone stood in front of them once more, the golden-hilted sword on the ground beside it.

'This is truly a wonder,' said Finlay.

'Indeed it is,' said the wise widow. 'I have never seen the like of it before.'

Finlay picked up the golden-hilted sword and they continued on their way, silently marvelling at what they had seen and done.

deaδLy δistuRBaNces

There was once a time when many a poor corpse in Scotland was denied the chance to rest in peace, for grave robbery was quite a common occurrence. There were two reasons to spend long, dirty hours in the sinister darkness of the graveyard. Firstly, there were the treasures to be found within the graves; rings and other items of jewellery might have been buried with the corpse, and sometimes, even the clothes could be put to good use. Secondly, there was a market for fresh corpses if you knew where to take them. Most of the customers were of the medical profession, eager to discover all they could about the workings of the human body, but it is said that there were also some customers who needed bodies for other, more sinister purposes, involving dark deeds and devilry of the worst kind.

Scotland's most notorious grave robbers were Burke and Hare, two labourers looking for an easy profit, who provided bodies for Dr Knox in Edinburgh. They soon grew tired of their nocturnal journeys to the cemetery, of course, and began to prey on the living, killing weak and vulnerable citizens of the capital themselves, thereby avoiding the loathsome toil of all the digging and the dirt. Burke was hanged for his crimes, but Hare escaped justice. Their story is true, even if it has acquired legendary status over the years. But there are many other stories that are told about the gruesome pursuit of the grave-robbers that leave their audience uncertain, for the historical facts behind them, if there are any, have never been proven.

And, as often happens, you might hear the same story more than once, identical in every respect apart from the place in which it is set and the names of the people who feature in it. The events in these stories may have happened once. They may have happened twice. They may never have happened at all, except in the imagination of the first person who told them, wherever and whenever that was. But as the stories are told and re-told, their entertainment value remains the same.

the minister's wife

The following story may originate in the north of Scotland, or in the Borders. It has also been said that the events that are recounted in it took place in a village in Fife.

The village minister was in deep mourning, for his wife had just died. She was a young woman, in the prime of life, and they had not long been married. It seemed desperately unfair that she should be taken from him so soon, leaving him alone. They had not even had a child together. All the villagers turned out for the funeral service, and when it was time for the burial, and the women had left, the menfolk had to fight back the tears as they followed the coffin on its final journey to the parish graveyard.

The minister bowed his head to hide his own tears as his wife's coffin was lowered gently into the grave. When the last of the mourners had gone away, he stayed by the graveside for more than an hour, lost in his grief. Then he walked away with shoulders hunched to join the wake.

There was quite a crowd at the funeral, and nobody noticed that there were two men in the village who did not attend the wake. Any feelings of sympathy they might have had for the young minister's loss were overridden by the tremendous greed of this unpleasant pair. They knew that the minister's wife had a wide band of solid gold on her wedding finger and they intended to take it. If they dug up the soft soil that lay on top of her coffin before it became compacted, their job would be all the easier, and so it was in their minds to act that very night, while the rest of the village were occupied with the wake. As soon as it was dark, they crept back to the cemetery, carrying their spades over their shoulders, and set to work.

No-one can deny that there is an eerie air about a graveyard at night, and the two men were nervous. Every sigh that the wind made in the trees made them jump. The noise of a hedgehog, snuffling in some leaves nearby, caused them great upset and they nearly abandoned their task. But they kept at it, working as quickly as they could to remove the earthen mound from the top of the coffin. They were soon standing in the grave itself, shovelling the earth up and over their shoulders to the edge. They tried not to think of the body lying beneath their feet and concentrated instead on working at a steady, even rhythm.

At last, their spades struck wood and they knew they were nearly there. They scraped the earth from around the coffin lid and after undoing the screws that secured it, prised it open. The minister's wife lay still and peaceful in her coffin, just as if she were sleeping, with her white grave-clothes arranged neatly around her outstretched body. On her left hand, which was clasped to her right and laid across her breast, a wide, gold band glittered in the moonlight.

The first robber shuddered. He had never become accustomed to the first sight of the bodies that they dug up. Some of the corpses looked almost alive, and it always made him edgy. But his companion had no qualms. He bent over the coffin, picked up the dead woman's left hand and started to pull at the wedding band. The ring would not budge. The robber pulled harder. The ring stayed right where it was, firmly stuck on the woman's finger.

'Here, you try!' said the first robber to the second. 'I can't get it to move!'

The second robber took a turn at pulling, but he got no further than his companion had.

'It's no use,' he said. 'I can't get it off. Let's give it up as a bad job and get out of here.'

But the first robber was not willing to give up so easily. He pulled a knife from his pocket, and started to hack at the corpse's finger, just below the ring. As he sliced through the white flesh, his companion turned his face away in disgust. The first robber carried on working with his knife, and within moments had completed the task. He held up the woman's severed finger in triumph for his friend to take a look. The second robber lowered his eyes, avoiding the grisly sight, and just as he did, he thought he saw a movement in the coffin.

'Look!' he gasped, white-faced, pointing at the minister's wife. The first robber looked, blanched and dropped the bloody finger he had been holding. This time there was no mistaking it. The corpse was stirring in its grave.

The two men moved faster than they had ever done in their lives before. Gasping and panting, they scrambled out of the open grave and fled. They carried on running until they were far out of the village. They could not stay there with a dead woman after them.

Back at the minister's house, the last visitors had gone and the minister was sitting alone by the fire. It had been a long and harrowing day. He lay back in his chair, closed his eyes with fatigue, and fell into a deep, dreamless sleep. Some time later, he was woken by the sound of knocking at the door. He rubbed his eyes and sighed. A visit at such a late hour could only mean one thing. One of his parishioners was in trouble, and he would get no more sleep that night. He got up and went to the door.

The sight that met his eyes when he opened it made him gasp, for there was his wife standing outside, dressed in a white gown and deathly pale. At first he thought it was a ghost. Then he saw the blood dripping from her left hand, and he realised what had happened. He picked her up and carried her inside, tears of joy running down his face.

the Living δеaδ

One winter's night, somewhere in the north of Scotland, two grave robbers were finishing their evening's work. There had been a funeral that day, and funerals meant business for the nasty pair. They knew of a man who paid well for fresh corpses, and this one was a fine specimen to take to him. It was the body of a man, neither very young nor very old, but not long dead and not yet decaying. The two men heaved the body into the back of their cart, covered it with a blanket, then closed the empty coffin and hastily shovelled the soil back into the grave, so that their thievery would not be discovered. Then they set off back along the road to the village.

Digging is thirsty work, and their throats were parched, so when they came to the inn at the edge of the village, they stopped, by mutual agreement.

'What about our cargo?' said one of them, nodding at the body behind him.

'Let him guard the horse and cart,' said the other with a wink. He took off his coat and climbed into the back of the cart. His friend helped him to dress the corpse in the coat, then added his own hat to the ensemble, placing it on the corpse's head at a jaunty angle. They pulled the corpse into the front of the cart and sat it up in the seat, with the reins in its hand and the blanket over its legs. When they had finished, the robbers smiled, for the corpse looked quite at home sitting there, its head bowed on to its chest as if taking a nap. Congratulating themselves on their ingenuity and wit, the two men went inside for a drink or two.

As the two robbers were entering the inn, two young men were just getting ready to leave. They drained their glasses, stood up, and went outside, staggering slightly with the effects of their evening's libations. When they got into the courtyard, they saw the horse and cart, with the man sitting at the reins.

'Good evenin'!' called out one of them in cordial tones.

'Aye, good evenin' tae ye!' boomed the other one cheerily. 'Cauld, though!'

There was no reply from the man in the cart.

'Are ye no goin' in for a dram?' enquired the first man.

The corpse said not a word, for of course, corpses can't speak.

Now, good spirits can easily dissolve into bad when the brain is befuddled with strong drink. The two young men took offence at the corpse's reticence. They advanced towards the cart with belligerent expressions. Then, when the corpse still did not move, one of them gave it a shove. The corpse keeled over to one side, and its coat fell open. The two men saw the shroud beneath the coat, and sobriety returned immediately. For a moment or two they stood still and stared at their discovery in silence. Then the first spark of an idea lit up the eyes of one of them. He beckoned his friend closer and whispered in his ear. With a mischievous laugh, his companion nodded, and they set about putting their plan into action. They pulled the dead body down from the cart and removed its coat and hat. Then they carried it over the road and heaved it over the wall into the field beyond. One of them put on the coat and hat and the other climbed into the back of the cart and hid. Then they waited.

The two robbers felt much better after a few drams. They would have liked to stay for a couple more, but they had a long drive ahead of them before they could complete their business. They left the inn and headed over to their waiting cart. The body in the front seat looked perfectly fine where it was, so they did not bother to return it to the back. They climbed up beside it and sat down, one on either side of it. One of them took the reins, and urged the horse into a trot.

They passed through the village and were soon travelling through open countryside. With his spirits soothed and his thirst quenched, the driver had drifted into a contented dream and was enjoying the ride. Then he heard a noise beside him. He laughed.

'Mind yer manners, Tam!' he said to his companion.

'It wisnae me!' complained the other robber. 'I was sleeping!'

'Aye, aye,' said his friend. Then he felt something push his right side.

'Stop shovin' me!' he said.

'I didnae shove ye!' said the other robber, who was beginning to get disgruntled. 'Quiet, now, I'm trying to sleep!'

The driver shrugged, and said no more. Then he felt something touch his leg. He looked down, and saw that one of the corpse's hands had slipped. He picked it up to move it back, and his heart leapt into his mouth.

'It's warm! It's warm! The body's warm!' he cried to his companion.

'Aye,' said the corpse in a deep, gloomy voice, 'this coat is very welcome on a chilly night like this!'

The young man in the back of the cart had to stifle snorts of laughter as the two robbers gasped at his companion's words. But the 'corpse' kept a straight face, and did not give the game away. The robbers leapt from the cart in terror and ran off down the road at full tilt, never stopping to look back. The 'corpse' and his friend were helpless with laughter as they watched their victims flee for their lives.

It was a wicked trick they had played on them, but it was no more than they deserved. There would be no profit from this night's work for the robbers, and with luck, the experience would steer them away from graveyards for good.

witcHes

Witches feature prominently in Scottish history and folk tales. For many years, magic, or the belief in it, was very much a part of life at all levels of Scottish society. From the late sixteenth century until the beginning of the eighteenth century, hundreds of suspected witches faced persecution, condemned by both State and Church as evildoers and servants of the Devil. Many hundreds went to their deaths, and the documents that remain, relating to the trials and prosecutions of alleged witches from all parts of the country, contain some details that seem quite fantastic. Many of the things of which these people were accused, particularly the many supernatural feats they were alleged to have performed, are more likely to have been reflections of society's beliefs about witches than testaments of witnessed fact. There are a great number of traditional tales about witches, and these tales reflect the same beliefs about the things that witches could do, good or bad, and the way in which they supposedly conducted themselves.

In 1591, a number of people from East Lothian were accused of witchcraft, and of using magic to threaten the life of King James VI. Written accounts of the events surrounding the trials and executions that followed included the information that, among other things, the accused had sailed to the kirk at North Berwick in sieves. In the story about the fisherman's wife and her friend on page 150, the belief that such a thing was possible is presented in fictional form. Witches were said to have the power of metamorphosis, or shape-shifting. Some of the North Berwick witches claimed to be able to change themselves into cats and another famous Scottish witch, Isobel Gowdie of Auldearn, who was tried in the seventeenth century, claimed she could change into a hare. Likewise, traditional tales are full of shape-shifting witches, who can change into cats, rats or hares, at will. The traditional tales are fantasy, but it is interesting to consider just how closely they mirror people's strange perception of reality in the period of the witch persecutions.

the witch of Laggan

A hunter had been out all day in the forest of Badenoch with his horse and his hounds. It was growing dark and a storm was brewing so he decided to take shelter in a bothy in the forest for the night. He tied up his horse outside, and took his two hounds into the ramshackle building with him, for they had worked hard that day, and had earned a warm place to sleep. He soon had a fire going, and made himself comfortable on a makeshift bed of straw, listening to the wind and the rain outside and feeling glad for the chance of a good night's rest.

Then he heard a scratching noise at the door. He got up to investigate, and when he opened the door, he found a bedraggled black cat outside. The hunter could see that the weather had taken a turn for the worse. The rain was coming down in torrents and the cat was soaking wet and shivering. Before the hunter could protest, the cat shot past him into the bothy, and cowered in a corner. The hounds snarled and snapped at the intruder. The hunter shouted at them to lie down, and they obeyed, but they lay with their eyes fixed on the scrawny black creature that had disturbed their peace, and from time to time, gave a low warning growl.

The hunter looked at the cat.

'Well, what are we to do with you?' he said. To his surprise, the cat spoke back. She confessed that she was a witch, but that she had fallen foul of the sisters in her coven, and now repented of her evil ways. She begged him to let her spend the night in the bothy, where it was dry, and promised she would be moving on in the morning.

The hunter was no lover of witches. He despised their evil ways, for he had seen the harm that they could do, and had circumstances been different, he might have been as glad to see the end of this witch as any other. But there was something about the pathetic creature shivering in the corner that roused his compassion, and he agreed to let her stay. The dogs continued to glare menacingly at the cat as she smoothed down her damp fur with her tongue, and when she raised her head to look back at them, there was fear in her eyes. The hunter beckoned her over to the fire to get warm, but she would not move.

'I cannot come to the fire, nor can I rest as long as these hounds are untied,' she said, 'for I am sure they are ready to attack at any moment. Take this hair, I beg you, and tie them to the roof beam securely, to give me peace of mind.'

The hunter took the hair from the cat, but he felt uneasy about her request, for she was a witch, after all. He wound the hair loosely round the necks of his hounds, and wrapped it over the roof beam, but he made only a pretence of securing it. Then he sat back down, and the cat moved over to sit in front of the fire. She stretched out and closed her eyes, and as she relaxed in the warmth from the flames, she seemed to grow. The hunter watched her apprehensively. A few moments later, he realised that she was indeed getting bigger, and a cold knot of fear formed in his stomach.

'You are getting bigger,' he said, trying to sound lighthearted. 'You are turning into a real beast!'

'Ach, don't worry,' smiled the cat. 'It's a grand fire you have going here, and the hairs on my back are puffing out as they dry in the heat, that is all.'

But the hunter kept his eye on her, and she grew some more, and as she grew, the hunter felt more and more afraid. The cat kept growing at a tremendous rate until she had reached a monstrous size. Then suddenly she was gone and the hunter saw a terrible witch standing in her place.

'You may well look scared,' she growled at him in a hoarse, coarse, voice, 'for I know full well who you are and that among your friends are some who have persecuted my sisters. Why only this morning, I saw your greatest ally, Macgilliecallum of Raasay. But he is dead now,' she said, with derisive laughter in her eyes, her voice adopting a tone of mock sorrow. 'And now,' she said, her voice rising to a shriek, 'I have come for you!'

The witch raised her arms and the hunter saw her long nails, curled like talons, ready to strike. He stood his ground and in a low voice, uttered a short word of command, and his faithful hounds sprang to their master's aid. The witch who had thought the dogs had been safely tied with the magic tether, was completely taken by surprise. The hounds pounced before she had a chance to protect herself. Their attack was swift and savage. They tore at the witch's legs and arms. Then they fastened their teeth into her breast. The witch tried to retaliate, beating at the dogs to try to get them to release their hold on her, but they could not be shaken off. These were hunting dogs, bred for their speed, strength and courage, and they would not give up. The witch moved towards the door, screaming with rage and pain as the hounds clung to her breast with their teeth. Only when she got outside the bothy was she able to shake them from her, and transforming herself into a great black bird, take off into the wind and the rain and the night. The hounds crawled to their master's feet, exhausted and bleeding. The hunter's heart was still pounding as he bent to stroke their heads and whisper his gratitude. But the struggle had been too much for the loyal hounds. It nearly broke the hunter's heart when he saw them slump to the ground at his feet and die.

The hunter buried the dogs and waited alone for the last few hours of the night before dawn broke. At first light, he set off for home. He rode without stopping until he could see the familiar outline of his house in the distance. He was longing to see his wife and to feel her comforting arms around him. But when he entered the house, there was no-one at home. Disappointed, he took some soup from the pot on the fire and sat down to wait. A short while later, his wife returned.

'Where have you been?' asked the hunter.

'I have been to call on the Goodwife of Laggan,' she said. 'She is very ill.'

'And what is the matter with the goodwife?' said the hunter, a little peevishly.

'She has been great pain since the middle of the night,' said the hunter's wife, 'and now she is at death's door.'

'And where is the pain?' said the hunter. He had suddenly become interested in the poor old woman's agonies. His wife pointed to her breast.

'Just here,' she said.

'And where does she live?' asked the hunter.

His wife told him.

The hunter said not another word. He left the house and jumped on his horse. Then he rode like the wind to the place his wife had described. There, in a tiny cottage overgrown with thorns and briars, he found the old woman lying on her deathbed, surrounded by anxious neighbours. He pushed his way through to the bedside, and threw back the blankets, exposing the bloody wounds on her breast.

'The woman whom you have all understood to be kindly and virtuous, and whose passing you have come to mourn tonight, is a witch!' he declared. 'It was she who killed Macgilliecallum of Raasay, and when she had done that, she came after me!' And he told them how he had tricked the evil woman, and showed how his dogs had left the marks of their attack on her body.

The witch raised her feeble head from the sickbed and spoke. 'My friends, I have deceived you horribly, but I beg your forgiveness,' she said. 'I have done many vile, wicked things, and I admit to you now that I was tempted by the Devil into his service. The full horror of all that I have done is now plain to me, and I must give you my confession in full, in repentance of my sins, and as a warning to all those who are tempted to follow the same path as I took.' In a weak and faltering voice, the witch then related the story of her seduction by the devil, and confessed to all the foul deeds she had done. When she had finished, her head fell back on the pillow and she died.

It was drawing close to midnight when not far from this terrible scene, two men, travelling along the road to Badenoch, caught sight of an old woman, hurrying towards them. As she drew near, they could see that she was in great distress. She was breathless and clearly in pain, and her clothes were torn and bloodied.

'How far to the kirkyard at Dalarossie?' she asked them, as she staggered by.

'Not far,' they replied.

'Will I get there by midnight?'

'If you hurry, you might make it,' they said, and wondered if they should offer to help her, for she was in a terrible state. But she would not have heard them, for she was already some way past.

Not long after their encounter with the old woman, the travellers came across two black dogs, also going in the opposite direction. The dogs ran past them whimpering with excitement, their tails high and their noses to the ground. It was clear they were on the trail of something. The dogs were followed by a man dressed in black, riding a black stallion. He stopped when he saw the two travellers.

'Did you see a woman on the road?' he wanted to know.

'Aye, we did,' said one of the men.

'Which direction did she take?'

'She was heading for Dalarossie Kirk,' said the man. Without another word, the rider urged the horse into a gallop, and passed by.

The travellers had not yet reached their destination when they were overtaken by the black rider, on his way back. In front of him, across the saddle of his horse, was slumped the body of a woman. Two black dogs clung to the bloody corpse. It was a chilling sight. The next day, the two men related their story to some local people. The people told them what they knew about the hunter and the Witch of Laggan. And the men realised that it was the dead witch they had seen, making a desperate bid to reach the sanctuary of the kirkyard before the Devil could claim her soul. She had been too slow.

the fisherman and the witches

There was once a fisherman who lived on the northern coast of Scotland. He was a God-fearing man, and lived an honest life. But the fisherman was married to a woman who did not share his pious thoughts. She stayed away from the church, and took to disappearing from the house at night when she thought he was sleeping, then sneaking back in just as the dawn was about to break. The fisherman suspected she was a witch, but he could not prove it and so he kept his thoughts to himself.

Then one night as he sat by the fire, a visitor came calling at the house. It was another woman from the village, who had come to see his wife. The two women sat in the next room and talked. They thought that no-one would hear what they were saying, but their voices carried into the room where the fisherman sat, and when he pressed his ear to the wall he could hear every word.

'So it's fishing tonight, is it?' said the visitor.

'Aye,' said the fisherman's wife. 'We'll have a great night's sport. Don't forget to bring the sieve!'

The fisherman thought they might mean to steal his boat, so that night when he went to bed, he closed his eyes and pretended to sleep, but he kept his ears open and stayed wide awake so that he would know when his wife crept out of the house. When she did, he got up and followed her. Out in the street, the fisherman's wife joined her friend, who was carrying a sieve, and the two of them started to walk towards the harbour. The fisherman followed a few steps behind, keeping himself well hidden in the shadows.

When they got to the harbour, the two women did not go near the fisherman's boat. He decided that perhaps they did not mean to take it after all, but he was curious to know what they were going to do, and so he stepped out of the shadows and challenged them.

'What are you doing out here in the middle of the night?' he asked.

The fisherman's wife was surprised to see him, but she was quite bold in her reply.

'Why, we're going fishing, that is all,' she said, 'and if you let us get on with it, we will bring you so many fish that you will not have to work for another week!'

'I should go with you,' said the fisherman, 'for the waters out there can be treacherous. And besides,' he added, 'I know a great deal more about fishing than you do.'

His wife laughed. 'You can't come with us,' she said. 'Stay where you are, if you like, and watch. You will be surprised to see just how many fish we can catch. But you must promise that whatever you see is kept a secret between us, and that you will not utter the Lord's name while we are out at sea.'

The fisherman made a solemn promise that he would say nothing. Then he watched. The two women went to the water's edge, and turned into rats. The rats climbed into the sieve, and sailed out onto the water. They sailed some way out from shore, but the fisherman could just make out the shape of the strange vessel by the light of the moon. Then the two creatures set to work. They steered the sieve round in a semicircle, like a dog herding sheep, and then turned back towards the shore. In front of them came a whole shoal of fish, their scales glittering like silver coins beneath the water. The fish swam up onto the beach and lay there in glistening piles before the fisherman's feet.

'Have we caught plenty fish?' came a voice from the boat.

'Aye, plenty!' the fisherman called back, stunned by the sight that lay before him.

But the rats were not yet satisfied. They turned the sieve round again and sailed out further into the distance and repeated the process. More fish landed on the beach.

'Have we caught enough yet?' called the voice from the boat. Donald looked at all the fish they had caught. If this went on much longer, there would be no fish left in the water for the other fishermen to find when they cast their nets the next day.

'More than enough!' he called out. 'More than enough!'

But the sieve sailed out to sea a third time, and a little while later, you could not see the sand for all the fish that lay on it. The fisherman began to get frightened.

The voice from the sieve called out to him again, 'Have

we caught enough fish yet?' And he knew he had to put a stop to it.

'In God's name, that's enough!' he shouted.

As soon as he had said it, he heard a cry out on the water. The sieve was filling with water and the two rats were drowning. The fisherman saw the little vessel with its devilish crew sink beneath the waves and knew that he had seen his wife for the last time.

the hunter and the hare

A hunter from the north was out riding with his hounds in the forest, and he caught sight of a hare. He called to his hounds to give chase, but they stopped, whimpering, and would not run after it. He spurred on his horse after the hare, meaning to catch it himself, but found all of a sudden that he was surrounded by a great number of hares, strange beasts that were completely unafraid of the horse or the dogs. They leapt and danced all around him, and he could not go any further. At once the hunter realised that these were no ordinary creatures and that they must be witches. It was common knowledge that a number of women in the district were involved in the devilish craft.

The hunter jumped down from his horse, cursing his dogs as useless creatures and lashing out at them furiously with his whip. Persuaded by this cruel treatment to take action, one of the dogs lunged at the biggest hare, which immediately took off, with its companions following. The hunter gave chase on his horse as the dog pursued the hare here and there through the forest. Then the hare turned and headed back towards him. It took a great leap into the air, as if it meant to jump right over the horse, and the hunter swung his sword, cutting off the hare's right forepaw cleanly at the shoulder. The hare ran off into the trees on its three remaining limbs, leaving a trail of blood behind it. There was no sign of the wounded animal's companions. They had vanished into thin air.

The hunter followed the trail left by the injured hare and discovered that it led to the home of an old widow, whom he knew was suspected of witchcraft. He went into the house and found her there. The woman's right arm was missing and she was desperately trying to stem the flow of blood from the terrible wound on her shoulder. When she saw the hunter she admitted at once that she was a witch and offered a full confession of her dreadful crimes, begging him for his forgiveness. But the hunter was in no mood for mercy. He dragged her from the house, resolved to take her to trial, and some days later, she was sentenced to death for witchcraft.

murder most foul

the Legend of sawney bean

The legend of Sawney Bean's life, grisly deeds and gory death is thought to have appeared in print for the first time at the beginning of the eightecnth century. A number of broadsheets were published in Britain containing accounts of Sawney's life, and the grisly deeds and gory death of his family. Copies of some of these broadsheets are still in existence. Although it was allegedly a true story, there were some inconsistencies between the accounts given, most notably regarding the time at which the events were said to have taken place. Efforts of researchers since then have failed to verify the story, and it is likely that the broadsheets were based not on historical fact, but on an older equivalent of the modern 'urban myth'. Nonetheless, fact or fiction, the legend continues to fascinate readers to this day.

Most versions of the legend set the scene in the reign of James VI of Scotland and I of England. Sawney Bean, according to the legend, was born in East Lothian. His father was a labourer, who made his living from hedging and ditching work on the farms around the district. His son was to follow in his father's footsteps, but soon found he could not tolerate the work and left home to look for an easier way to make a living. He soon took up with a woman who was of like mind, and they moved together to the wilds of Galloway, where they found a cave by the sea in which to live. They were to stay in the cave for some twenty-five years, their clandestine activities causing widespread puzzlement, fear and alarm.

Sawney and his wife's chosen means of supporting themselves was by murder and robbery. They preyed on passing travellers, ambushing them on lonely stretches of wayside. Having killed their victims in cold blood, they removed the bodies to the safety of their cave, thereby evading detection. But concealment of the bodies was not their only purpose, for human flesh was also good meat for the Beans. They dismembered the corpses, and cut the flesh into pieces. That which was not to be eaten at once was pickled. Occasionally, when they had a surfeit, they carried excess body parts some distance along the coast and cast them into the sea. From time to time a rotting limb would be carried in by the tide and be washed up on the beach, where it would be discovered, much to the consternation of the people who lived in the vicinity.

The Bean family grew; Sawney and his wife had children, and their children had children, all the products of incestuous relationships within the family. The Beans did not mix with the rest of society. And as the family grew, so its murderous industry increased. Some of the unfortunate victims of the Beans were people in transit, passing through from one place to another, and their presence in the area, having never been noticed, was not missed. But others lived in the district, and over the years, as the number of missing persons grew, so did the fear of the locals. A number of brave souls were sent out along the routes that the victims had taken to see what they could find. Those that were fortunate enough to return came back with neither clue nor information. Clutching at straws, the people pointed accusing fingers at innocent pedlars, or innkeepers along the road. Some men were sentenced to death, only to have their innocence proven too late when the Beans had spirited away yet another victim. And now that there were more of them, the Beans did not need not to confine their attentions to solitary passers-by. Two, three or even four people could disappear at one time. Search parties were sent out along the coast, but found nothing. The Beans were well hidden in their cave, which went far into the rocks at the shore. At full tide, the cave mouth flooded, and it was assumed by people who passed nearby that no-one could conceal themselves in it. But deep within its cavernous interior, where the water did not reach, the Bean family was safe, and dry.

It was only by chance that Sawney and his family were discovered. For the first time in all these years, one of their victims survived to tell the tale. A man and his wife were riding back from a fair one day when they were ambushed by the Beans. The man's wife was dragged from her horse and set upon by the women of the terrible clan. They cut her throat, and slaked their thirst on her blood before starting to butcher her lifeless body. Meanwhile, the man struggled fiercely with his attackers, who ducked and dodged to avoid his flailing sword and the hooves of his terrified horse as they tried to get a grip on some part of him to pull him down. Then, just as the man was weakening and it looked as if he would be slaughtered too, a crowd of people appeared over the brow of the hill, on their way home from the fair. The Beans saw them coming and ran off, leaving the remnants of the woman's bloody corpse some yards away in their flight. The man hurried towards the approaching crowd and told them what horrors he had experienced. He showed them what remained of his wife, and they were shocked beyond belief. The man was taken at once to Glasgow, from where the magistrates sent messengers to the king, and the hunt began in earnest.

The king himself took command of a large body of troops, to ride to the spot where the incident had taken place. The man who had so narrowly escaped guided the party along the route he had taken, and a search along the coastline was set up, with hunting dogs called into service to flush out the cannibals. The party rode along the beach at low tide, and the riders missed the mouth of the cave in the rock face. But the dogs had caught the scent of human flesh and stopped. When they saw the dogs run yapping and baying into the gloom of the cavern, the hunters turned, and backtracked. They lit torches to see better in the darkness, and went in mob-handed. Not one of them could have been prepared for the sight that greeted them.

In the deepest recesses of their hidden lair, the whole Bean clan was in residence, snarling and growling like the animals they had become. All around was evidence of their barbaric existence; piles of clothing, jewellery, weapons, money and other belongings of their victims. Numerous human body parts, hung up to dry, festooned the walls, while still more lay pickled in tubs of brine. It was a sight that would haunt its discoverers for the rest of their lives.

For once, the Beans were outnumbered, and could offer no effective resistance to their hunters. They were captured and bound with all speed. Then after their human spoils had been given some form of burial, they were marched back to the capital to face justice. News of their coming spread rapidly, and the streets of Edinburgh were lined with curious onlookers as the Beans were brought to the Tolbooth. Their guilt was proven beyond doubt, and no time was wasted in declaring their sentence, which was carried out within twenty-four hours. Not one member of the family escaped justice. They were all, men, women and children of all ages, sentenced to death. They were taken to Leith, where the female members of the family were made to watch as the men and boys had their limbs amputated and were left to bleed to death. Then the females were burned alive, and the smoke from the fires that consumed them cast a great, grey cloud over the port.

tHe muRδeR HoLe

Merrick Moor was a bleak and desolate place to be at the best times. People did not walk there for pleasure; only those travellers whose shortest route lay across its rugged landscape ventured out on it, and few made the journey alone. Without a companion to cheer you, you could find yourself eerily alone for hours on end, with only the cries of the curlews and the sigh of the wind to break the silence. And in recent years, the moor had developed a more sinister air, for first one person, and then another had set out across its unforgiving landscape and never returned. As time passed and the number of missing persons grew, so the rumours spread. Some people thought that the lost souls had sunk in a marsh somewhere; others blamed supernatural forces; but most people believed that evil deeds were being done, somewhere out there, although by whom they could not tell.

The pedlar boy knew all about the rumours, and he

hesitated before he set out that night, but he had a bundle of wares to sell and needed to get to the next village for market day. With a sinking heart, he shouldered his pack and started out on his journey under a darkening sky.

Soon a storm had blown up, and the boy found himself struggling to make headway against the wind. With each gust, it sent sharp needles of icy rain darting into his face, making his eyes smart, and hacking at the skin of his cheeks until it was raw. Every so often, a noise would startle him; a crack of thunder, the cry of an owl. It dawned on him that out here, all alone, he was utterly defenceless, and his imagination began to run riot. But it was too late to go back, and too cold to stop, so he gritted his teeth and walked on, singing songs under his breath in an effort to keep his mind off the discomfort and fear. Then he looked up, and saw a cheering sight. In the distance, a light winked at him, beckoning him towards it. The pedlar boy remembered that the last time he had passed this way, he had found lodgings in the house of an old woman and her two sons, who took in passing travellers and gave them food and a bed for the night in exchange for a modest sum. He had stayed there in the company of some others on that occasion, and they had found the family to be quite hospitable. They appeared to have taken a particular liking to the young pedlar, for when he had been gathering his things ready to leave the next day along with the other guests, the old woman had tried to persuade him to stay a while longer. As another chill blast struck him full in the face, the boy made up his mind that he would go on no further. With head down against the rain, and chin tucked into his chest, he made for the lights of the cottage ahead.

He knocked at the door, at first tentatively and then with greater force, but no-one came to answer. He knew there were people at home, for he could hear sounds coming from within. Thinking they could not hear his knocking for the noise of the storm, he went to the window from where the light was coming, and looked inside. The three occupants of the cottage were all there, but were too busy to notice his presence. The old woman was on her hands and knees, scrubbing the stone flags and spreading sand all around where she had cleaned. Her sons were hunched over a great chest in the corner, cramming a large, bulky object into it. The boy watched the men as they leaned on the lid of the chest to force it shut, and locked it. Then he knocked on the window, to alert them to his presence.

The poor lad did not get the reception he had been hoping for. The door of the cottage was flung open, and the two brothers dragged him inside, a knife to his throat. Thinking that they took him for a robber, he stuttered out his innocence before they could do him any harm.

'You must remember me,' he said, 'for it is only a few months since I last stayed here for the night. I am only a poor pedlar boy, looking for shelter from the storm!'

The brothers released their grip on the boy's arms, and their mother glared at him.

'Are you alone?' she asked him.

'Yes,' the boy said, 'and I have never felt so alone as I did tonight out on that moor. I have heard too many tales about strange happenings in these parts, and I wish I had never set out on my journey tonight.'

Slowly, the old woman's mouth twisted into some semblance of a smile, and she relaxed.

'Come over to the fire,' she said, 'and warm yourself. Hang your wet clothes to dry, and I will fetch you some supper.'

When he had eaten, the boy felt a little better, but there was something about his hosts' manner that made him uneasy, and a small knot of apprehension began to twist inside him. And when he was shown to his bed in the adjoining room, the knot grew bigger. The room was in total disarray. The blankets from the little box bed were strewn on the floor and the curtains around it, ripped and ragged, hung by a few thin threads. Over by the window, the table and chair had been knocked on their sides. The chair had lost one of its legs and the table top was scratched and splintered at the edges. The door could not be locked, for the bolt had been forced and broken.

The sight of all this chaos did nothing to soothe his frayed nerves, but the poor lad was tired out from his lonely trek across the moor, and wanted nothing more than to close his eyes and sleep, so he determined to put his fears to the back of his mind. He did what he could to set the room to rights, then he lay down on the bed to rest, leaving the candle burning beside him for some comfort.

Finally, his body relaxed and he fell into a restless sleep, but his dreams were visions of terror, punctured by cries and groans from unseen creatures, and they kept the fear alive in his mind. He had not been sleeping long when he was woken with a start by another cry, this time a real one, and the sound of people moving about. The sounds were coming from the next room. The boy peered across the room to the gap under the door. With horror, he watched a dark, sticky stream of blood trickling across the stone flags in the next room towards his bedroom door. He crept from his bed and opened the door a fraction. Through the gap, he could just make out the figures of the two brothers, hunched over something on the floor. One of them held a bloody knife in his hand. They stepped back and the boy heaved a sigh of relief when he saw that the blood had come from a goat, which lay with its throat cut on the floor. Cursing himself inwardly for his foolish imagination, the boy was about to return to his bed when his ears picked up the thread of the men's conversation, and he froze.

'If only all the throats we cut were as easy as this,' said one.

'Aye, said the other, 'We've had some difficult customers.'

'What about the boy?' said the first. 'Do you think he'll put up a struggle?'

'He should be no trouble', said the first. 'I'll see to him in a bit.'

'Why bother with the mess and the blood in here?' asked his brother. 'Let's do him at the Murder Hole. Quick, clean, one wee splash, and he'll disappear for ever. He'll be dead in a second, and off down to join the others. It's so deep in there, there must be room for hundreds more, and they'll never be found.'

'Right enough,' said the first brother. 'Do it the easy way. Then we can see what's to be got from that tidy bundle he carries with him.'

The boy did not stay to hear any more. Without even taking the time to gather up his pack, or put on his boots, he made for the window. He was as quiet as he could be, but panic made him clumsy as he squeezed through the window. He was careless in the way he jumped, and stumbled when he landed on the ground outside. As he staggered to his feet and started to run, he heard one of the brothers giving the alarm, and calling for the bloodhound. He knew he would be very lucky if he could escape with his life, but he was not going to give up without a struggle. He stumbled across the shadowy moor in the darkness, heedless of the stones that cut into his feet, and the heather scratching his bare legs. He could hear the hound coming close behind him, and the angry shouts of the two brothers following it. Raw terror gave strength to his tired legs, and forced them on across the uneven terrain, through the marsh, over the rocks, up the hillside and across the burn.

He staggered on blindly, conscious only of the need to keep moving forward, until he came to a scree-filled dip in the ground. The ground gave way under his feet and he fell forward, ripping the skin from his face, hands and knees on the sharp stones. He lay there for a moment, motionless. The pain from his wounds made him want to cry out, but the fall had winded him badly and he had no breath left in his lungs. He knew that the hound was getting closer by the second, and he prepared himself to die. Then his breathing returned in a great, agonised gasp, and with it came his instinct to live. He forced himself to his feet and scrambled out of the dip, then lunged on into the darkness ahead.

The hound caught the scent of the fresh blood from the pedlar boy's wounds, and baying with excitement, increased its pace. But when it reached the spot where the boy had fallen, it stopped. The two brothers came panting up behind it and shouted for it to move on. They kicked it and beat it, but nothing would persuade it to go any further.

Without the hound to lead the way, the two men knew that they would never find the boy in the wilderness that lay ahead. They gave up the chase and returned to their cottage, snarling with fury at their useless beast.

It was morning when the boy finally reached the nearest town, faint with cold and fatigue. The skin on his feet was torn to shreds, and the cuts from his fall were dirty, inflamed and encrusted with dried blood. He knocked at the door of the first house that he came to, and when the door was opened, he collapsed inside. Once he had been cleaned and fed and dressed in warm clothes, he recovered enough strength to give an account of his ordeal of the night before. The description that he gave of the old woman and her sons was so accurate that the people knew at once who they were. There were several villagers who had lost friends or relatives on the moor in recent times, and their astonishment at the pedlar's pitiful condition turned to murderous rage when they heard what he had to tell them. A large party gathered together and set off at once to get their revenge. They found a horse for the pedlar boy, to save him from walking, and he rode along with the crowd.

The old woman and her sons were dragged from the cottage, screaming for mercy and protesting their innocence. But when they looked at the crowd that had come to find them, and saw that the pedlar was among them, they realised that their time had come. As three gibbets were hastily erected on the hillside, the murderous family offered a full confession of their crimes. They reckoned they must have killed almost fifty people, and had dropped almost every one of them, dead or dying, into the fathomless depths of the Murder Hole.

Only one of their victims had not yet been consigned to the watery grave, for he had only been killed the night before, and his body was still in the cottage, hidden in a chest. When he heard this, the pedlar boy realised with a shudder what it was he had seen when he had looked in at the window. The murderers directed their captors to the spot where their terrible secrets lay concealed; a small dark pool concealed in the long grass some distance off. Somewhere in there, too far down for them ever to be recovered, were the remains of all the people who had gone missing in that lonely wilderness.

The crowd was quick to dispense justice. Although there were some among them that would rather have seen the murderers torn to pieces, it was agreed that a lawful execution should be carried out. The sentence of death was duly declared and the woman and her two sons were hoisted up on the gibbets. As the crowd turned to go, leaving the three bodies swinging in the wind, the pedlar stroked the warm neck of his horse, and listened to the murmur of people's voices, and was thankful. He was still in the land of the living. A couple of seconds slower in his flight, and he would have been gone; far down, out of sight, keeping company with the dead in the Murder Hole.

taLes of the cLans

There are hundreds of tales of the clans of Scotland, stirring stories of loyal clansmen following their chiefs into battle, tales of rivalries and feuding between different clans over land and honour, tales of virtue and valour and tales of murder and treachery. Many relate to real events, but have been embellished and romanticised, while some may have no basis in historical fact, but are legends which were developed not only to entertain but also to glorify the name of the clan and keep alive the memory of the chiefs in its past.

the Loch of the sworð

The Loch of the Sword, in Gaelic Lochan a Chlaidheimh, is a small loch approximately a mile from Rannoch. In the early years of the nineteenth century, the loch was depleted by drought, and a local boy spotted a rusty claymore in the shallow water. The sword was taken to Fort William for further examination, and might have become an exhibit in some museum or other, had it not been for the intervention of the men of Lochiel. On their insistence, the sword was returned with great ceremony to the loch where it had been found. For the sword had a history, and its place in the loch was a symbol of peace after a long and bitter struggle for land, three centuries before that.

Land was a precious commodity, and the Chief of the Clan Cameron, Ewan Cameron of Lochiel, had long been contesting ownership of certain lands around Rannoch with the family of Atholl. Negotiations failed, and acts of aggression had solved nothing so far. At length it was agreed that Lochiel and Atholl would meet by the Loch of the Sword to settle matters once and for all. Each man was to take only one other with him.

On the appointed day, Lochiel set off for the Loch of the Sword with his piper to accompany him. On the way to the meeting place, he was stopped by an old woman. She was a witch, who went by the name of the Blue-eyed One.

'Where are your men, Lochiel?' she said.

Lochiel explained to her that he needed no more men with him, for he was going to meet Atholl, who would also have only one other for company. But the old witch persisted.

'Where are your men, Lochiel?' she asked him again. 'It is a wolf you are going to meet, and you will need your hounds with you. Turn back, and fetch your finest men.'

Lochiel could not ignore the warning. He turned back from whence he had come to fetch a bodyguard, and when at last he faced up to Atholl by the Loch of the Sword he had fifty strong men to protect him, hiding in amongst the heather nearby.

Atholl and Lochiel debated long and hard, but time passed and although their voices became louder and their arguments more forceful, neither would give way. At last, Atholl lost patience. He waved his hand and drew his sword. This was a signal, and within seconds, twenty of his men came out of hiding close to where the two chiefs stood.

'Who are they?' demanded Lochiel.

'They are Atholl sheep, come to graze on Lochiel's pastures,' said Atholl.

Lochiel threw aside his woollen cloak and drew his sword. This was his signal. Instantly, fifty fine men came storming towards the loch to stand by their chief.

'Who are they?' asked Atholl.

'They are the dogs of Lochiel, come to feast on the sheep of Atholl,' replied Lochiel. 'They are fierce, and hungry for blood. If you value the lives of your sheep, you should remove them from my land.'

Atholl knew that Lochiel had got the better of him, and agreed to surrender his claim to the grazing lands. As a token of his word, he took his sword and pitched it into the middle of the loch. The lands would belong to Lochiel until such time as the sword was recovered.

the faerie flag of the clan macleod

The Macleod clan still has its seat on the Isle of Skye, in Dunvegan Castle. The castle and gardens attract a large number of visitors every year. One of the most fascinating things on display in Dunvegan castle is the Faerie Flag, a tattered, brownish piece of cloth with faded red markings, displayed proudly in a glass case. Although it is not much to look at, the legend of the Faerie Flag ensures that it is more proudly and carefully preserved than any other treasure belonging to the Macleods.

According to the legend, there was once a handsome young chief of the clan who had reached the age when he might marry, but had not yet found a bride. There was no shortage of young women who were prepared to become his wife, but none of them found favour with the young chieftain. It seemed as if he would never find a partner to share his life, until one day he met a beautiful young woman and fell immediately head over heels in love with her. To his delight, it seemed that the young woman felt as strongly about him as he did about her, and he soon asked her to marry him. The young woman then told him that she was no mere mortal, but a fairy princess, and would have to ask her father, the king, for his permission before she could consent to marry him.

The princess approached her father with the news that she had fallen in love with a mortal and wanted to become his wife. The king was not unsympathetic to his daughter's plight, but explained that he could not give his permission for such a union to take place, as it would only bring her heartbreak. Fairies lived for ever, but her beloved Macleod was only human, and would eventually die as all humans do, leaving her to grieve eternally over the loss of him.

Macleod and the princess were distraught at the thought of having to part from each other so soon, and so the fairy king took pity upon them and gave them his permission to be married to each other for one year and one day. After that time, he would bring the fairy horde to the bridge near Dunvegan Castle and claim her back, and the two must part.

The two lovers spent a blissful year together at the castle, and towards the end of the fairy princess's stay there, a beautiful baby son was born, making their happiness complete. But they knew that their time together must come to an end, and exactly one year and one day after they had been married, the fairy king appeared with all his people at the bridge, just as he had promised, waiting for the return of the princess. The chieftain held her tightly as she wept in his arms, preparing to bid farewell to him. As she got ready to go, she made him give her one promise; that he should never leave their child to cry. If the child was left to cry, the sound of his wails would reach her in the land of the fairies and would cause her terrible anguish. The chieftain gave her his word that he would do as she asked.

After kissing her son and her husband goodbye, the fairy princess walked over the bridge to join her people who were waiting at the other side. The chieftain bowed his head and wept, and when he looked up again, his young wife had disappeared.

Time passed and the chieftain sank into a terrible depression. Nothing could pull him out of the deep pit of despair into which he had fallen. The only time he showed interest in anything was when he was playing with his son, but even then, his eyes were full of sadness rather than laughter.

The chieftain's followers eventually decided that something had to be done to lift their master's spirits, and so they decided that a great party should be held in the castle. Surely the sound of the pipes and the company of clansmen and friends would cheer him. The chief's birthday was approaching, which was a good opportunity to call for a celebration, and so, with the reluctant agreement of the grieving Macleod, preparations were begun at once for the big night.

Macleod's birthday party looked set to be a great success. There was music, singing, dancing and plenty of fine food and drink. The assembled company was in fine spirits and before long, the chieftain found himself swept up in the gaiety of the occasion and joining in the dancing.

Upstairs in the castle, a young nurse had been employed to take care of the chieftain's baby. The baby was an easy and contented child, and she had no difficulty settling him down to sleep. She should have stayed with him as she had been ordered, but the sound of the revelries downstairs was irresistible and, thinking that the child would sleep soundly throughout, she left the room to watch the party from the top of the stairs for a short while.

While the nursemaid was away, the child became restless in his sleep, and kicked off the blanket that was covering him. It was a chilly night, and soon afterwards, feeling cold and uncomfortable, the child woke up and began to cry. His cries grew louder and louder, but outside in the hallway, his nursemaid was caught up with the sights and sounds of the festivities below her, and the music was so loud that neither she, nor anyone else in the castle, could hear him. Far away, in the hidden world of the fairies, the sound of the baby's crying reached the ears of his mother, and she could not bring herself to ignore such a piteous sound. She slipped away from the fairy kingdom and returned to the human world to help her son. When she appeared in the castle, unseen by any of the humans present, and discovered the party in full swing, she realised what must have happened. She picked up the baby from his cradle, comforted him with whispered, loving words and shushed him to sleep in her arms. Before she laid him down in his cradle again, she took off her own silken shawl and wrapped it securely round him to keep him warm. Then she kissed him gently and vanished into the night.

When the nursemaid returned to the baby's room and found him peacefully sleeping, but wrapped in a strange shawl, she was perplexed. Eventually, she confessed to the chieftain about her absence from the baby's room and showed him what she had found on her return. Macleod was as puzzled as she was, but no harm had come to the baby and so the shawl was put away and no more was said on the matter.

Some years later, when the child was older, he told his father that he remembered his mother's visit to him on the night of the birthday party and repeated to him the words she had whispered in his ear that night. The shawl was a magical fairy flag, which could be used to protect and preserve the clan Macleod. If the clan faced possible extinction for any reason, the Faerie Flag could be taken out and waved three times, and the danger would pass. The flag could only be used three times, however, and once it had been called into service on three occasions, its magic would no longer work.

It is said that the Faerie Flag has been used twice so far. It was handed down from one chieftain to the next and kept in a casket that never left his side. For many years it was unused, until one day, the Macleods found themselves surrounded by the clan Donald in battle and seriously outnumbered. The chief knew that without supernatural intervention, his men faced certain death and so he took the Faerie Flag from its casket and waved it three times. No sooner had he done this than the Macleod ranks were swelled by hundreds of the fairy folk, making it appear to the opposing clan as if they had been suddenly outnumbered ten to one. The Donald warriors took fright and retreated, and the Macleods were saved. On the second occasion, the cattle of the clan were struck down with a terrible disease and were all dying. Winter was coming and the members of the clan faced starvation and death without meat or milk. The chief of the time realised that the clan could be wiped out within a year unless something was done and so the Faerie Flag was taken out for a second time. As soon as it was waved, the Fairy folk descended upon the lands of Macleod once more and healed all the ailing beasts with a touch of their swords.

There has never been call for the Faerie Flag to be used since that day, but it may be that its magic works in other ways. During the Second World War, members of the Macleod clan who took part in the Battle of Britain took photographs of the Faerie Flag with them in their wallets for good luck. Many British airmen perished in the terrible battle of the skies, but none of the Macleods lost their lives.

There are plenty of people who are ready to dismiss the legend of the Faerie Flag as pure romantic fantasy, who will argue that it is a mere rag, a tattered relic of the crusades around which a fanciful story has been concocted. Nonetheless, it is preserved faithfully by its owners as a talisman, ensuring the preservation of a proud and noble Scottish lineage.

the war of the one-eyed woman

The following legend tells how hostilities broke out on the Isle of Skye between the Macleods of Dunvegan and the Macdonalds of Sleat. Rory Macleod of Dunvegan had a sister, named Margaret, and it was agreed that she would be hand-fasted for a year to Donald Gorm Mor Macdonald of Sleat. Hand-fasting was commonly practised in the Highlands of Scotland. It acted as a kind of preliminary to a marriage contract. The man and woman involved lived as man and wife during the period of hand-fasting, but if the pair proved to be incompatible, the arrangement could be dissolved at the end of one year. In theory, hand-fasting had the merit of preventing many an unhappy marriage but in practice, it could cause great upset, bitterness and in some cases, deadly enmity between the two families involved in the arrangement.

It may reasonably be assumed that when Margaret Macleod set off from Dunvegan to join Donald Gorm Mor at his home at Duntulm, hopes were high on both sides for a long, happy and fruitful union. But this was not to be. In the first place, poor Margaret lost an eye during her stay there, and her beauty, thus marred, no longer lived up to Donald Gorm Mor's high expectations. Secondly, after twelve months of living with Donald Gorm Mor as his wife, Margaret showed no signs of producing a child.

When the year was up, Donald Gorm Mor decided that the union was not to his liking, and that Margaret should be sent back to Dunvegan. He underlined his rejection of the poor woman in a particularly insulting manner, by arranging for her to make the journey on a one-eyed horse, accompanied by a one-eyed man and a one-eyed dog. Not surprisingly, Rory Macleod of Dunvegan was outraged at Donald Gorm's cruelty and leapt to defend his sister's honour. The resulting hostilities were called Cogadh na Cailliche Caime – the War of the One-Eyed Woman.

holy men of scotland

saint fillan of glen dochart

Saint Fillan, a son of Feriach, a Munster prince and Saint Kentigerna, was born in the eighth century in Ireland. He came to Scotland as a missionary with his mother and brothers. Kentigerna moved to Loch Lomondside, and Fillan, after some years as abbot of a monastery on the Holy Loch in Argyll, moved to Strathfillan in Glen Dochart, to build a priory near Auchtertyre. It is said that as Fillan was working on the construction, he used an ox to help with carrying materials, and ploughing the land. A wolf attacked the ox and killed it, and Fillan reproached the animal, explaining the holy nature of the work that the ox had been doing. The wolf was so filled with remorse that it offered to work in place of the ox, so that the building work might be completed.

Close to the site where the priory built by Fillan once stood is the Holy Pool, which is said to have been blessed by the saint. It was believed to have healing powers, and to have been particularly effective in the treatment of insanity, and for many years, people with mental illness would travel to Strathfillan to bathe in its waters. Saint Fillan travelled around Scotland, visiting the Western Isles, Perthshire, south-west Scotland and Fife. He also spent some time living as a hermit in a cave at Pittenweem, which is named after him. It is thought that he lived until old age and when he died, his body was buried at Strathfillan. He used his holy powers for healing the sick, and had eight healing stones, which he left to his followers on his death. The stones have very distinctive shapes, and each one was used for a different part of the body; the head, the abdomen, the back and the limbs. Saint Fillan's healing stones are still in existence, and are kept in the Tweed Mill visitor centre in Killin. Many people who visit believe that the stones still have curative properties, and touch them or rub them in the hope of relieving pain or disease.

After Saint Fillan's death, his left armbone and hand were preserved by his followers as a relic. It was said that while Fillan was studying to become a monk, his left arm lit up to allow him to read by its light, so that he could study late into the night. Centuries after Saint Fillan's death, in 1314, Robert the Bruce asked for the relic, known as The Mayne, to be brought to Bannockburn. The custodian of the relic feared for its safety and brought only the empty box, firmly locked, hoping that he would not be found out. But as Bruce was saying his prayers the night before the battle, he heard a noise coming from the box and asked the custodian to unlock it. When the custodian opened the box, he was astounded to find that Fillan's arm had found its way back inside. He confessed to Bruce that he had brought an empty box with him, and that the reappearance of the arm was miraculous. The king took courage from what could only be a sign from God, and was inspired to victory.

Another relic of Saint Fillan is his bell, known as the Bernane. It is now in the safekeeping of the Museum of Scotland. This bell was supposed to come to the saint whenever he called it. It is said that the bell was cracked when a startled hunter saw it flying through the air and shot at it with his bow and arrow. The bell was stolen and taken to England in the late eighteenth century, but was recovered in 1869 by Bishop Forbes of Brechin, who returned it to Scotland. Saint Fillan's staff, the Quigrich, is kept along with the bell in the Museum of Scotland.

saint mungo

Saint Mungo, founder and patron saint of Glasgow, was born in the sixth century, in extraordinary circumstances. According to Jocelin of Furness, who documented the life of Saint Mungo six centuries later, Mungo's mother was Thenew, a daughter of Loth, a prince after whom the region of Lothian was named. Thenew became pregnant after being raped by Owain, Loth's nephew, and her father was enraged. He had her thrown from the top of Traprain Law in East Lothian, and then, seeing that the fall had not killed her, ordered that she be cast adrift in the Forth in a coracle. The boat drifted across the Forth to the Fife coast, and landed at Culross, where Thenew gave birth to her child.

Saint Serf, who ran a religious community in Culross, found the mother and child and gave them his protection. The child was named Kentigern, which means 'head chief', but Saint Serf gave him another name, Mungo, meaning 'dear one', and it is by this name that he is most commonly known. Mungo was raised and educated by Saint Serf in Culross. One of the miracles associated with Saint Mungo relates to this period of his life. Saint Serf had a pet robin, which was killed by some ruffians. Mungo found the dead bird and restored it to life.

When Mungo reached adulthood, he was invited to Strathclyde by the king. He was consecrated as a bishop and lived by the Molendinar Burn, where he built his first church. Glasgow Cathedral now stands on the site of Saint Mungo's original church. According to tradition, the site for the church was chosen not by Mungo, but by God. Mungo had come across Saint Fergus, who was dying, and had lifted him into his cart. He instructed the oxen pulling the cart to take it where God willed it to go, and the oxen took the cart to the Molendinar Burn. When Fergus died, Mungo buried him there and began construction of his church. After about thirteen years, Mungo was compelled to leave Scotland because of religious disputes and moved to Wales to continue his work. There, he founded a monastery at Llanelwy.

Around 570, he returned to Scotland at the invitation of King Roderick of Strathclyde and settled in Dumfriesshire for some time before returning to Glasgow. Here, according to tradition, he performed the miracle for which he is best known. Roderick's wife, Langoureth, was unfaithful to her husband. She gave her lover a ring that Roderick had given to her. A servant of the king discovered the affair and told the king about it. The king was enraged, all the more so when he saw that the guilty man was wearing the ring he had given to his wife. Instead of confronting the couple with their sins, he determined to trick them into a confession. He stole the ring from the man's finger while he slept, then threw it into the river. Then he asked his wife where the ring was. When she could not produce it, he threatened to kill her unless she found it within a specified period. Langoureth sent a plea to Mungo, asking for his forgiveness and begging for his help. Mungo sent one of his monks to fish in the Clyde, telling him to bring back the first fish that he caught. When the monk returned with a salmon, Mungo cut it open, and there, safely tucked inside the fish, was the king's ring. He sent it back to Langoureth, who presented it to a very surprised King Roderick. Roderick had no choice but to take back his accusations.

Glasgow's coat of arms recognises the saint that founded the city and gave it its name, 'Glesca', meaning 'dear place'. Depicted on the coat of arms are the bird that Mungo restored to life, the salmon in which the ring was found, and the ring. And the motto of the city is derived from one of Saint Mungo's sermons. 'Let Glasgow flourish by the teaching of the word,' said Mungo. The city's motto is 'Let Glasgow flourish.'

saint andrew

Unlike Saint Mungo and Saint Fillan, Saint Andrew did not live and work in Scotland, and the legend relating to his connection with this country originated many centuries after his death.

Saint Andrew is the patron saint of Scotland. He was a fisherman who became one of the twelve disciples of Jesus, and he carried on the work of Jesus after the crucifixion, preaching the gospel in Syria and Asia Minor. He was put to death in Greece by Roman soldiers, and according to tradition, was crucified on a diagonal cross. His relics were taken to Constantinople, but they were moved from there in the fourth century. It is said that most were taken to Italy, but that Saint Regulus took some bones to Scotland, to the place which was to become St Andrews, in Fife. The bones are no longer in existence, and it is thought that they were lost during the Reformation, but a plaque in the ruins of St Andrews Cathedral marks the place where they were once kept.

Although 30th November, Saint Andrew's Day, is still not celebrated to any great extent in Scotland, it is marked as a special day both in Scotland and in several countries around the world where ex-patriots or people of Scottish descent have congregated. The saltire, the national flag of Scotland, is a white diagonal cross, representing the cross upon which Saint Andrew was crucified, on a blue background. The story of how the St Andrews cross came to be adopted as Scotland's flag dates from the ninth century AD.

There was conflict between the Picts and the Scots and the Northumbrians during this period, over control of the area around Lothian. In 832, an army of Scots and Picts were preparing to do battle against the Northumbrians at Athelstaneford, in East Lothian. The night before the battle Angus McFergus, the leader of the Picts, had a vision in which Saint Andrew appeared before him, promising him victory the next day. The next day, in the midst of the fighting, Angus looked into the sky and saw an x-shaped cross appear in the clouds overhead. He remembered the vision of the night before and took heart. The sight of the cross gave his men great inspiration, and they fought their way to victory. The white cross, against a blue background representing the sky, was adopted by the Scots as an emblem of their nation from that day.

the Glaistig and the Kelpie

Highland folklore is animated by a wide variety of supernatural creatures, either harmful, or benevolent, and there are countless tales of man's encounters with them, some tragic, some humorous, some romantic. Two such creatures that feature in a large number of stories are the *glaistig* and the *kelpie* (*each-uisge*, or water-horse).

The glaistig was always female, a tutelary being who was believed to dwell in lochs and rivers, and to have a special attachment to animals and young children. When she did make herself visible to the human eye, it was said that she appeared as half-woman, half-goat, or as a woman with long fair hair, clothed in green. She watched over sheep and cattle, saving them from straying into danger. Often, as the adults went about their daily chores, the glaistig kept the children entertained with fun and games. It was commonly thought that glaistigs could attach themselves to particular families, as guardian spirits. In many parts of the Highlands offerings of milk or food were often left out for the glaistig to ensure that her loyalty to those under her protection remained steadfast. There was another side to the glaistig, however. She could tease and torment, and sometimes, she could do harm. The story of the glaistig's curse illustrates this belief.

The kelpie, water-horse or *each-uisge*, was another water-dwelling creature. It was widely thought to be malevolent, capable of luring many innocent souls to their deaths in its sub-aquatic lair. Although it was sometimes said to have the power to transform itself into the shape of a man, it generally appeared on land as a magnificent horse and tempted weary travellers to try to ride upon its back. Once they had mounted, they found that they could not dismount and were dragged, helpless, underwater by the kelpie. There they would be devoured. Sometimes evidence could be found of the victim's fate. It was generally thought that the kelpie did not eat all of its victims, but left a small part of them – the liver, some said, or the heart – and these would be washed up at the water's edge where searchers could find them. One story tells of a number of children who encounter a kelpie while playing at the water's edge. All but one of them climb on the creature's back. The last child reaches out to stroke the creature's head, and as his first finger touches it, it becomes stuck fast. The child draws his knife and cuts off his finger in order to save himself but can only stand and watch as his companions disappear beneath the waves on the kelpie's back. In another version of the same story, six little girls are lured on to the kelpie's back, but the seventh child, a boy, is too cautious to risk it. The kelpie tries to catch him, but he manages to escape. Most kelpies appeared as black horses, but the River Spey was thought to be the home of a kelpie that took the form of a great white horse. The deaths of many people who drowned in the river's white-flecked, tumbling waters were blamed upon the kelpie. The majority of stories about kelpies depict this mysterious creature at its worst; a mortal enemy of man, who may sometimes be outwitted, but should always be feared. The story of the kelpie of Loch Garve on page 187 is different.

the glaistig of ardnadrochit

There was once a glaistig who lived in Ardnadrochit on the Isle of Mull. She was a guardian of the Lamont family and looked after all the cattle that belonged to them. She was devoted to her duties. One day, as the glaistig was out herding the cattle, she saw some men approaching. They were cattle raiders from Lorne, and they had come to steal the beasts away from her. The glaistig could not move the cattle fast enough to get them to safety, but she would not allow the raiders to take them away. She struck the animals on their backs with her magic wand, and turned them all, one after another, into great grey stones, which are still lying where she left them.

The glaistig had foiled the thieves but the loss of her animals broke her heart and there was nothing that the Lamont family could do to console her. She pined away and died, and they buried her close to the stones.

the glaistig's curse

There was once a man named Kennedy, a big, strong blacksmith from Lochaber. He was travelling home one night on his horse and just about to cross the ford of the river, when a glaistig sprang up in front of him. She wanted a ride on his horse.

'Would you not be the better of a rider behind you?' she asked him in a teasing voice.

'A rider before me would be better,' declared Big Kennedy, and so saying, he swept up the glaistig with one arm and sat her on the saddle in front of him. He had a magic sword belt with him and with this, he circled the glaistig's waist and his own, and held her captive.

'Let me go! Let me go!' she shrieked.

'What will you promise me if I let you go?' demanded Big Kennedy.

'I will give you a herd of fine strong, beautiful speckled brown cattle,' she crooned, 'and I will promise you success whenever you go hunting!'

'All very fine,' said Kennedy, 'and it will do for a start, but it is not enough. What else will you promise me?'

'I will build you a new house,' she said, 'and it will be a fine house — the strongest house you could ever hope to have; safe from storm and flood, invincible against attack by man, beast, fairy or any other creature.'

Kennedy was impressed. 'Do all that you have promised before the morning,' he said, 'and I will let you go free.'

The glaistig called out in her strange, shrieking voice and summoned all the magical helpers she could to carry out the work she had promised. They worked with a speed and efficiency that was a wonder to behold, cutting and fetching the strongest roof timbers, hewing great, square, straight-edged stones from the hillside and passing them one to another to the site where the house was to be built. They laboured on through the night, piling up the walls, heaving the door and window lintels into place and cementing the stones together, fixing on the roof beams with a battering of nails and weaving on the thatch at a great rate. When they had finished, the blacksmith had a fine house indeed, complete with a new workshop and forge. The fire burned brightly, and the heat of it warmed the cold night air for miles around.

Then the glaistig cast the spell to protect the building from anything that might endanger it, and the first part of the work was done. In the short time that was left before dawn broke, the helpers constructed a new cattle fold beside the house, and in the very last minutes of darkness, disappeared and reappeared, each one leading a fat, speckled cow, heavy with milk, into the fold.

Kennedy was pleased with the work.

'Now,' said the glaistig, 'will you let me go?'

Kennedy undid the buckle on the magical belt and the glaistig stepped out of it, stretching her aching limbs. 'Farewell, Kennedy, you have profited well from your meeting with me, but now that I am done with my tasks, I must take my leave.' But Kennedy was not willing to let her go free to torment other travellers crossing the ford. As the glaistig raised her hand in farewell, he reached into the fire and pulled out a white-hot branding iron. He pressed it into the glaistig's hand, burning away the flesh and sinew right down to the bone. She gave out a scream loud enough to shake the trees in the next county. Then she ran to the top of a nearby hill, and standing on a boulder on the summit, shrieked out a curse in revenge for her injury.

Grow like rushes,
Wither like fern,
Turn grey in childhood,
Change in height of your strength;
May not a son succeed.

The glaistig shrivelled to nothing, leaving a blood red stain on the hillside. But her curse lived on after her.

The smith grew frail and grey-haired before his time. He had a family, but all the children aged quickly and became weaker as they grew. His sons died before they could marry and have children. It was a heavy price to pay for a new house and a herd of cattle.

the keLpie of LoCH ɢaRve

The kelpie of Loch Garve lived in a cold, dark, underwater lair, hidden from sight in the very deepest part of the loch. He liked his home just fine, and although he ventured onto land from time to time, he was always glad to get back to familiar surroundings, where his wife waited for him. But the kelpie's wife was not happy. She felt the cold terribly, and life in the lair was miserable for her as she shivered and shook, trying, and failing to get warm. She complained to her husband, but he did not feel the cold like she did, and at first he thought that she was just making a fuss over nothing.

Time went on, and the kelpie's wife became more and more unhappy. At last, he realised that if he wanted to keep her, he would have to do something to make the place a little more comfortable for her. He left home the very next day, and swam to the surface of the loch, where he turned himself into a beautiful horse. Then he went to the house of a man he had heard of, a builder who knew how to construct all sorts of useful things. When he got to the builder's house, he stamped on the ground until the man came out. The builder was surprised to see such a beautiful horse on his doorstep. It seemed to be waiting patiently for him to mount it, and so he climbed on. As soon as the builder was sitting upon his back, the kelpie took off like the wind. The builder was terrified, for he realised that he was stuck fast to the kelpie's back, and they were heading towards the loch. He muttered a silent prayer as the kelpie plunged into the water, and he felt himself going down, down into the cold and dark. But the kelpie did not want to harm him. When they got to the bottom of the loch, he let the builder dismount. Then he explained his problem to him.

He told him how his wife could not get warm in their home deep down in the loch, and how unhappy she was. And he asked the builder to help. If the builder could make something to help the kelpie's wife get warm, then he would be able to return safely to dry land, with a promise of a plentiful supply of fish from the loch to eat, whenever he wanted it.

The builder set to work at once, and made a great big fireplace in the kelpie's lair, with a great big chimney to carry the smoke to the surface of the water. When the work was complete, and the fire was lit, the kelpie looked at the smile on his wife's face with pleasure. He returned the builder safely to his own home on dry land, and true to his word, kept the kindly tradesman supplied for the rest of his days with plenty of fine, fresh fish from the loch.

They say that even in the coldest of winter weathers, when all around is frozen, there is one small area of water on Loch Garve that stays free from ice. That is because far below the surface, a fire is burning merrily in the kelpie's home, and the heat which rises up from it stops the water on the surface from freezing.

the killing of the kelpie of raasay

There was once a blacksmith who lived on Raasay. He owned a number of cattle and some sheep, and from time to time, one of the beasts disappeared. The smith knew that the likely culprit was the kelpie who dwelt in the loch nearby. He was angry, but felt that he could do little to stop it happening. Then one day the kelpie went too far. The smith's daughter had been out working with the animals that day, and she did not return home at the usual time. Evening turned into night and still there was no sign of her. The smith waited anxiously for many hours, then as soon as the dawn came up, he went with his son to look for her.

When they reached the edge of the loch, they found the girl's liver lying amongst the pebbles and realised at once that the kelpie must have taken her. The smith's fury knew no bounds. He made up his mind to destroy the creature. With the help of his son, he lit a great fire at the water's edge, and used it as a makeshift forge to make a number of large iron hooks. Then the two men set up a spit on which they put a sheep to roast. As the sheep's carcass began to cook, sending an appetising aroma over the waters of the loch, the smith set the hooks in the fire to heat until they were red-hot.

The greedy water-horse caught the scent of the cooking meat and surfaced. It swam over to the fire and made a grab for the sheep's carcass with its jaws and as it did so, the smith and his son set about it with the red-hot hooks. At last it was dead, and they turned away, leaving its inert body lying on the shore. The next day, the smith and his son returned to the lochside but could find no trace of the kelpie's body. All that was left by the ashes of the fire was a heap of starshine.